Mark-André Krogeı

Database Mining

Mark-André Krogel

Database Mining

Propositionalization for Knowledge Discovery
in Relational Databases

VDM Verlag Dr. Müller

Imprint

Bibliographic information by the German National Library: The German National Library lists this publication at the German National Bibliography; detailed bibliographic information is available on the Internet at http://dnb.d-nb.de.

Cover image: www.purestockx.com

Publisher:
VDM Verlag Dr. Müller Aktiengesellschaft & Co. KG , Dudweiler Landstr. 125 a, 66123 Saarbrücken, Germany,
Phone +49 681 9100-698, Fax +49 681 9100-988,
Email: info@vdm-verlag.de

Zugl.: Magdeburg, Otto-von-Guericke-Universität, Diss., 2005

Produced in USA and UK by:
Lightning Source Inc., La Vergne, Tennessee, USA
Lightning Source UK Ltd., Milton Keynes, UK
BookSurge LLC, 5341 Dorchester Road, Suite 16, North Charleston, SC 29418, USA

ISBN: 978-3-639-01419-8

Acknowledgements

This thesis would not have been possible without all the help that I received from many people.

First of all, Stefan Wrobel was a supervisor with superior qualities. His kind and patient advice made me feel able to climb the mountain. He even saw good aspects when I made mistakes, and I repeatedly did so. I will always be very grateful for his support, and I take his positive attitude as a model for myself.

Then, there were so many teachers, colleagues and students of influence in my years at Magdeburg University and Edinburgh University, that I cannot name them all. Thank you so much!

I am also grateful to the friendly people of Friedrich-Naumann-Stiftung, who generously supported my early steps towards the doctorate with a scholarship and much more.

Last not least, my family was a source of constant motivation. So I dedicate this thesis to my children, including a citation I wish they will remember.

Und wenn ich weissagen könnte,
und wüßte alle Geheimnisse und alle Erkenntnis,
und hätte allen Glauben,
also daß ich Berge versetzte,
und hätte der Liebe nicht,
so wäre ich nichts.

1. Korinther 13, 2

Contents

List of Figures

List of Tables

Abbreviations

The following table lists frequently used abbreviations, for the convenience of the reader.

Table 1: Frequently used abbreviations in alphabetic order

3E	Effectivity, Efficiency, and Ease of use
CNF	Conjunctive Normal Form
DBMS	Database Management System
DDB	Deductive Database
DHDB	Deductive Hierarchical Database
DT	Decision Tree
ECML	European Conference on Machine Learning
FOL	First-Order Logic
IG	Information Gain
ILP	Inductive Logic Programming
MDL	Minimum Description Length
KDD	Knowledge Discovery in Databases
MRDM	Multi-Relational Data Mining
OLAP	On-Line Analytical Processing
PKDD	European Conference on Principles and Practice of KDD
PMML	Predictive Model Markup Language
RDB	Relational Database
ROC	Receiver Operating Curve or Characteristic
SQL	Structured Query Language
SVM	Support Vector Machine
UR	Universal Relation
WH	Working Hypothesis

In most cases, abbreviations are explained when they first occur in the text.

Chapter 1

Introduction

1.1 Subject of the Thesis

The amounts of data stored for many different purposes e.g. in business and administration are growing rapidly. Technical opportunities and legal necessities are among the reasons for this development. Knowledge Discovery in Databases (KDD) represents a chance to exploit those masses of data beyond the original purposes, for the extraction of valuable patterns. Many institutions regard KDD as an important factor in the economic competition.

KDD projects have shown that large investments have to be made especially for data preparation, i.e. before automatic analysis can take place. One of the reasons is a gap between the formats of data in operational systems and archives on the one hand, and demands on data formats as used by widespread KDD systems on the other hand.

Many information systems rely on database management systems (DBMS) for storing and manipulating data. Especially, relational databases (RDB) have reached a high maturity and widespread use. Here, data are held in a number of related tables, together with meta-data that describe tables and other aspects of a database. Actually, predicate logic or first-order logic is found at the theoretical and historical roots of relational databases.

Conventional systems for KDD demand for a single table as input, where each object of interest is described by exactly one row, while columns contain values of certain types which describe properties of the objects. Here, relationships among objects are neglected. The expressive power of this representation formalism for data — and formalisms for the knowledge to be learned from that data — corresponds to the expressivity of propositional logic.

A group of approaches to bridge the gap described above evolved over the last years: methods for propositionalization. These approaches transform a multi-relational representation of data and even knowledge in the form of first-order theories into a single relation, which can serve as input for conventional KDD algorithms. This transition from a representation with the expressive power of predicate logic to the realms of propositional logic is responsible for the name of the group of approaches, which are in the focus of this thesis.

Propositionalization quickly turned out to be a valuable approach to learning from relational data, even compared to more direct approaches to learn first-order theories as usual in the area of Inductive Logic Programming (ILP). However, traditional approaches to propositionalization remained complex and subject to high information loss in the course of the transformation.

In this thesis, we investigate opportunities for both effective and efficient propositionalization, which should also be easy to achieve for the analyst. This is done within a new framework for approaches to propositionalization, which also helps to unify descriptions of the traditional approaches.

The main objective is partly to automatize steps of data preparation for KDD and partly to enable the analyst to systematically accomplish data preparation. Ultimately, this is supposed to decrease costs. We work with the assumption that propositionalization can enrich the spectrum of methods available for data analysts in a valuable way.

1.2   Goals and Contributions of the Thesis

With this thesis, we aim at answering the following general research questions in the context of propositionalization:

1. How can approaches to propositionalization be described in a unified way in a formal framework?

2. How can aggregate functions serve propositionalization to be more effective?

3. How can further database technologies serve propositionalization to be more efficient?

The relevancy of answers to those questions was already hinted at. Relational data, especially relational databases, are a widespread means for managing data in many institutions. Data preparation for relational data mining is costly, since it has to be accomplished by experts in the domain to be analyzed and in KDD. Effective, efficient, and easy to use tools such as those for propositionalization could help here significantly.

Good answers to the questions seem non-trivial, which can already be seen in the diversity of approaches to propositionalization. Ideas to use universal relations (UR) are not helpful in most cases, since URs show a tendency to grow exponentially with the number of relations in the database they are derived from. Moreover, URs would usually contain more than one row for each learning example and thus not be suitable as input for conventional data mining algorithms.

Traditional approaches to propositionalization show high complexity and thus problems with scalability or high information loss endangering effectivity. We present an approach developed within our framework that achieves a good point in the spectrum of quality of learning results, on the one hand, and efficiency of their computation, on the other hand.

We answer the questions posed above in Chapters 3, 4, and 5. In the latter two chapters, further more specific questions are derived and developed into working hypotheses that are finally empirically investigated. All experiments were performed especially for this thesis, largely in a unified way. With this focus on experimental results, this thesis is in the general tradition of machine learning research, which provided much of the basis for KDD, and more specifically in the tradition of the dissertation by Kramer [58].

Similar to Kramer's work, we propose a new approach to propositionalization. Differently, we do not develop a new ILP method to learn first-order theories. Rather, we compare the results of different approaches to propositionalization, among them our own approach, to several well-known ILP systems from other sources. We use a larger number of data sets and learning tasks from as different domains as chess, biochemistry, banking, insurance, and genetics. Data set sizes are of different orders of magnitude. We further simplify the usage of declarative bias by using meta-data as provided by the DBMS. We apply ideas suggested by Kramer for the setup of our empirical work. Ultimately, we can confirm and enhance Kramer's positive findings on propositionalization.

1.3 Overview of the Thesis

After this introduction, we provide in Chapter 2 an overview of the basics that are relevant for the understanding of the kernel chapters of this thesis. Among those foundations are central ideas from KDD, RDB, and ILP. A focus is also put on general aspects of data preparation for data mining.

In Chapter 3, we present our framework for the unified description of existing approaches to propositionalization, especially those that evolved within ILP. We apply the framework for a detailed investigation into those traditional approaches, which is supposed to provide the reader with the opportunity to better understand the original presentations and to compare the approaches at an abstract level.

We continue in Chapter 4 with a new approach as an instance of our framework. The approach is influenced by ideas prominent in the area of RDB applications, viz. the usage of aggregate functions. We compare our results to those achieved with the help of popular ILP systems and other systems for propositionalization.

Chapter 5 explains further measures that we take to enhance our approach, especially for further improving effectivity, efficiency, and ease of use. Here, we continue series of experiments from the preceding chapter to complete the picture of up-to-date propositionalization.

Finally, Chapter 6 presents conclusions and our ideas for further work. Appendices provide further details of the software applied in our empirical investigations, about the data sets and learning tasks used for the experiments, including example scripts and log files, and an illustrative example database.

Chapter 2

Foundations

This chapter provides a concise introduction — or rather a reminder — to the basics of the following chapters. We chose a style that we hope is easy to read. Especially, we did not repeat many of the formal details that may be found in text books or other introductions to the relevant areas of research. We expect that for computer scientists, many concepts will be familiar. For people involved in KDD, most terms will be in their everyday use.

For further convenience of the reader, we provide two means: a running example for illustrative purposes, to be found right before the list of references to the literature at the end of this thesis, and an index pointing to the explanation of important notions in our text right after the references.

2.1 Knowledge Discovery in Databases

2.1.1 Data and Knowledge

Confronted with the term KDD, it is plausible to ask for the meaning of component terms, especially those of "data" and "knowledge". We do not intend to provide a philosophical discussion of these concepts here, but rather point to a view as formulated by Borgelt [15]. There, *data* are characterized as

- referring to single instances such as single objects, persons, events, points in time etc.

- describing individual properties

- often available in large quantities, e.g. in databases or archives

- usually cheap to get, e.g. from supermarket cash registers with scanners or from the Internet

- not allowing us to make predictions

Example 1 *In our running example, which we will use throughout this thesis and which can be found in Appendix D, each row in a table contains data in the sense of the above characterization. For instance, line 1 in table* T *refers to some object and describes it as* pos *with this value for its attribute* T_cl. *This is supposed to mean a positive class label, here.*

Further, Borgelt describes *knowledge* as

- referring to *classes* of instances such as *sets* of objects, persons, events, points in time etc.

- describing general patterns, structures, laws, principles etc.

- often desired to be concise

- usually expensive to get, e. g. by education

- allowing us to make predictions

Example 2 *In the running example, the observation of the distribution of class values for the* T *objects would result in a piece of knowledge. It allows for a so-called default prediction for* T *objects that do not show a class label, viz. the majority class label seen so far.*

2.1.2   Knowledge Discovery as a Process

From descriptions of data and knowledge as provided above, it is obvious that knowledge can be of higher value than data, which clarifies a part of the motivation for KDD. This concept should be defined now more precisely.

We cite one of the broadly accepted definitions, originally given by Fayyad and colleagues [32], and in a similar spirit also provided by many other authors, here a choice in alphabetical order by first author: Berry and Linoff [10], Han and Kamber [37], Hand and colleagues [38], Witten and Frank [132], and Wrobel and colleagues [134, 136].

Definition 1 Knowledge Discovery in Databases (KDD) *is the non-trivial process of identifying valid, novel, potentially useful, and ultimately understandable patterns in data.*

Example 3 *Thus, the determination of proportions of class labels for* T *objects, cf. Example 2, would* not *qualify as KDD, since it can be computed in a trivial way. Positive examples for KDD follow below.*

The relevance of the demands put on patterns to be found by KDD seems self-evident. Further explanations may be found in the literature. Essential for the definition is the concept of KDD as a process. There are a number of process models to be found in the literature, among them the CRoss-Industry Standard Process for Data Mining (CRISP-DM), cf. `www.crisp-dm.org`. Similarly, Wrobel [134] distinguishes phases mainly intended to

- understand the application and define objectives

- obtain and integrate data from source systems, including pre-analyses and visualization

- prepare data for analysis by sampling, transformation, cleaning

- choose methods for analysis

- choose parameter settings and run analyses

- evaluate and clean results, including visualization

- use results, e. g. in reports or operational systems

A typical KDD project will not complete these phases one after the other but regularly revisit earlier stages for adaptations of the corresponding steps and results. The central step of actually running the analyses is often called *data mining*. In other contexts, data mining is also used as a synonym for the whole KDD process.

A relevant point is the distribution of costs among the KDD process phases: the largest part is usually spent here in the first phases, especially for data preparation. For instance, Pyle [101, p. 11] provides a figure of 60% of the overall project time to be spent on data preparation. This highlights the relevance of the central issue of this thesis with its objective to support data preparation for data mining.

2.1.3 Tasks for KDD

An important part of data preparation is the construction of a suitable input for data mining systems. Typical data mining algorithms expect their input to be in the form of a single table. Rows of such a table represent the objects of interest. Columns represent attributes or features of those objects, for which values are given in the table. Most data mining components of the large commercial environments for data analysis belong to this group of typical systems.

One may also adopt the view that each object of interest is described here by a vector of its feature values. Considering independent objects of one kind only, the expressive power of the representation of examples (data), and also of the representation of patterns to be found by KDD (knowledge), remains equivalent to the expressive power of propositional logic, cf. Subsection 2.3.1. We come to define a notion to encompass those typical data mining systems, which we also call *conventional* data mining systems.

Definition 2 *A* propositional learning system *takes as input a single relation, i. e. a set of tuples of feature values, where each tuple describes an object of interest, and on this basis computes and outputs patterns in the sense of the KDD definition.*

The tuples referred to in Definition 2 are called *learning examples* and denoted by E in the following. They reside in a so-called *target table* or *target relation*. If the target table includes a special attribute, whose values should be predicted based on other information in the table, this attribute is often called the *target attribute*.

Typical tasks for data mining to be solved with the help of propositional learning systems are

- classification: learning systems determine patterns from learning examples with class labels; patterns have the form of classifiers, i. e. structures that can be applied to unlabeled examples to provide them with class labels

- regression: similarly to classification, unseen examples are equipped by learned patterns with additional numeric information

- clustering: objects of interest are grouped such that members of a group are similar, while members of different groups are not similar

- association rule discovery: subsets of objects with certain properties such as frequency of common occurrence are in the focus here

Especially association rule discovery has been very prominent in the field of data mining, starting with work by Agrawal and colleagues [2]. A popular field of application for association rule learning is shopping basket analysis.

However, we concentrate in this thesis on a special case of classification, viz. for two-class problems, which is also known as concept learning. Since we deal with a special case of learning functions from examples here, we provide a definition given by Wrobel and colleagues [136] for the general case.

Definition 3 *Let X be a set of possible descriptions of instances (i. e. examples without function values such as class labels), D a probability distribution on X, and Y a set of possible target values. Further, let L be a set of admissible functions, also called hypothesis language. A learning task of type* learning functions from examples *is then the following:*

Given: a set E of examples in the form $(x, y) \in X \times Y$, for which holds $f(x) = y$ for an unknown function f.

Find: a function $h \in L$ such that the error of h compared to f for instances drawn from X according to D is as low as possible.

Since f is unknown and may be obscured by noise in the data as well, one often tries to estimate the true error considering error rates for labeled examples that were not seen during learning.

A reason for our focus on binary classification problems, i.e. with Y being a set of two values, are the good opportunities to evaluate learning results in this scenario. Moreover, it is a basic case, where methods for its solution can also be generalized to other kinds of learning tasks.

Actually, our proposals are not restricted to concept learning, as we will also demonstrate. However, some ILP systems that we use for comparisons are restricted to this learning task or equivalents. So, for reasons of comparability and uniformity, we restrict ourselves to two-valued target attributes here.

Learning for classification and regression usually depends on example descriptions containing target function values. This is also called *supervised learning*. Clustering and association rule discovery usually do without class labels or similar information. They are examples of *unsupervised learning*.

2.1.4 Algorithms for KDD

A large variety of algorithms for the discovery of knowledge in several forms has been developed in the last decades. Among them are the very prominent approaches to decision tree learning, developed in the fields of both statistics, e.g. by Breiman and colleagues [19], and machine learning as a part of artificial intelligence / computer science, e.g. by Quinlan and colleagues [102]. Further methods include rule learning, among others influenced strongly by Michalski [82].

If demands for the comprehensibility of patterns are relaxed, we can also count a number of further methods to the spectrum of KDD approaches. For instance, approaches from the large field of artificial neural networks [111, 39, 16] can be used for classifier learning. The same holds for the younger field of support-vector machines, which is based on work in statistics by Vapnik [127], with an excellent tutorial by Burges [20], and many interesting results, e.g. by Joachims [49, 50].

Further, there are instance-base methods, genetic approaches, and the field of Bayesian learning to be mentioned, also well-explained by Mitchell [84]. This list does not even cover the wide range of methods for clustering and other central tasks of KDD. However, instead of extending the hints to the literature, we present one of the approaches in more detail and apply it to our running example: decision tree learning.

As the name suggests, the intention is to arrive at knowledge in the form of decision trees here, i.e. induce certain structures from example data. In a widespread variant of decision trees, such a structure contains zero or more inner nodes, where questions about attributes of the examples are asked, and edges corresponding to answers to those questions.

The edges finally lead to leaf nodes, each of which is associated with a class label. In a first stage of decision tree learning, such trees are built from labeled examples, considering this class information. In a later stage, these trees can be used to classify unseen examples. We concentrate in the following on the tree generation phase.

In essence, a set of examples should be recursively partitioned here such that the final partitions contain examples for one class only, if possible. Partitioning is achieved w.r.t. the attributes of the learning examples. Here, it is essential to use methods for the evaluation of attributes w.r.t. their ability to form the basis for good partitions. Usually, these methods are heuristic in nature.

One of the prominent criteria is information gain (IG), suggested by Quinlan [102]. We explain IG in more detail here since we use it in later chapters. Mitchell [84] gives the following definition for this criterion, here with an adopted nomenclature, with E being the set of learning examples and A a nominal attribute with the set of possible values $V(A)$

$$IG(E, A) \equiv H(E) - \sum_{v \in V(A)} \frac{|E_v|}{|E|} \ H(E_v) \tag{2.1}$$

E_v is the subset of the learning examples that show value v for attribute A. H stands for entropy, a measure from information theory, here for the impurity of a set of examples w.r.t. class membership. It is defined as

$$H(E) \equiv \sum_{i=1}^{c} -p_i \ log_2 \ p_i \tag{2.2}$$

where p_i is the proportion of elements of E belonging to class i. In the case of concept learning, we have $i = 2$.

Information gain can be regarded as the expected reduction in entropy when the value for the attribute in focus is known.

Example 4 *Imagine an extension of table* T *from the running example as depicted in Figure 2.1.*

The entropy of the set E of the 10 examples as given in table T *w.r.t. the class or target attribute* T_cl *amounts to about 0.97. The evaluation of* T_cat1 *shows that for all three values of the attribute, the corresponding subsets E_v are class pure such that their entropies are zero and thus $IG(E, T\_cat1) \approx 0.97$. Note that $0 \ log_2 \ 0$ is defined to be 0 here.*

For T_cat2, *the entropy of E_s amounts to about 0.81, that of E_t to about 0.65, and the weighted sum of these entropies to about 0.71, such that $IG(E, T\_cat2) \approx$*

T				
T_id	...	T_cat1	T_cat2	T_cl
1	...	m	s	pos
2		n	s	neg
3		m	t	pos
4		n	t	neg
5		o	s	pos
6		o	s	pos
7		n	t	neg
8		n	t	neg
9		n	t	neg
10		n	t	neg

Figure 2.1: Table T of the running example in an extended variant

0.26. *This is clearly less than for* T_cat1, *such that the first attribute would be chosen for partitioning in this step of tree building. Actually, because of the pureness of the partitions, no further steps are necessary. The small resulting tree can be depicted as in Figure 2.2.*

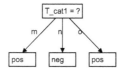

Figure 2.2: An example decision tree (four nodes incl. three leaf nodes)

Note that if class purity would not have been reached with just one question, further partitionings of the respective subsets of examples could have been carried out.

For numeric attributes, information gain can be computed with respect to certain threshold questions in the inner nodes of decision trees, e. g. greater-than tests, for partitioning the set of examples. Furthermore, note that information gain is only one representative of many heuristics in this field.

2.1.5 Further Relevant Issues

An important issue to mention here is *overfitting*. Decision trees and many other kinds of patterns can be constructed in a way to perfectly model training data. However, this often captures aspects that are not in general valid for the whole population the training data were drawn from. Thus, classifications for unseen data can suffer from those over-complicated trees.

A prominent method to reduce effects of overfitting with trees is pruning. Pruning uses test data with known class labels, which were not used for building a tree, to evaluate branches of the tree and cut them off in case of low value. Then, leafs assign class labels according to majority votes, i.e. the class label most prominent among training examples sorted to that leaf, for example.

A final *evaluation* of such a model can be achieved using validation data. Again, those data must not have been used for building or pruning the tree, but include class labels, to compare those labels with the predictions of the tree. For such a prediction, a validation example is sent from the tree's root to the leafs, corresponding to the answers of the example to the questions in the inner nodes. The prediction is read off from the leaf node where the example arrives. In the same way, unseen examples with unknown class labels get classified.

The process of the construction of a decision tree as a form of a model or *hypothesis* can be regarded as a *search* in the space of possible hypotheses. Here, search starts from a tree that poses no restrictions on the examples and thus predicts them all to belong to the majority class, for instance. Search proceeds by introducing heuristically chosen conditions on examples, thereby extending the hypothesis. This way, examples may be differentiated into several classes.

For details on hypothesis spaces with a general-to-specific order, which can be exploited during search, the reader is referred to Mitchell [84]. We return to this subject for refinement operators as mentioned in Section 2.3.

Furthermore, sophisticated methods have been developed to deal with *imperfect* data, e.g. containing missing values, within decision tree learning and also other propositional learning systems.

Moreover, especially in data mining, aspects of *efficiency* have always played a predominant role, with suggestions e.g. of special data structures for decision tree learning by Shafer and colleagues [118]. Overall, propositional learning systems have reached a high degree of maturity which makes their application to real-life problems possible and desirable.

2.2   Relational Databases

Relational databases are among the most prominent means for the management of data, e.g. in business and administration. In this section, we list key concepts and methods in this area, which are of relevance for our work.

2.2.1   Key Concepts

In the preceding section, there were already concepts of relations or tables mentioned, further those of objects and their attributes or features. These are central concepts for relational databases as well. Here, a basic means for modeling parts of our real-world perception are *relations* as sets of tuples of values from certain domains.

Figure 2.3 provides an impression of these concepts in the context of our running example with table T as extended above, following a figure by Heuer and Saake [41, p. 20]. For more formal descriptions, the reader is also referred to the book by Abiteboul and colleagues [1].

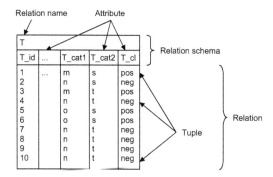

Figure 2.3: An illustration of central concepts of relational databases

On such a relation, a number of operators can be applied. One prominent operation is *selection* to produce a subset of the tuples that fulfil certain conditions w. r. t. their attribute values, i. e. to extract rows from the table. Another prominent operation is *projection* to reduce tuples to certain elements, i. e. to extract columns from the table.

Furthermore, arithmetic operations can be applied to one or more numeric attributes of the table to manipulate existing columns or to produce new ones. For attributes of different types, e. g. for string or date values, there exist special operations within most DBMS.

Note that all values for an *attribute* must be of the same type, a marked difference from other widespread means for data storage and manipulation such as spreadsheets. The term *feature* is often used as a synonym of attribute, which we also do in this thesis.

So far, we remained in the realms of adequate inputs for KDD with looking at single tables. Now, we go beyond that and consider systems of tables, as typical for relational databases. Here, different tables usually describe different kinds of objects, which can be related in some way. Relationships are modeled in relational databases with the means of *foreign key relationships*.

It is common to have at least one attribute (or a combination of attributes) in each table, the value of which is different for each tuple in the relation. Such an attribute can serve as a so-called *primary key attribute* for that table. An attribute in a table, which can take on values chosen from those of the primary key attribute of another table, is a so-called *foreign key attribute* and constitutes a foreign key relationship between the two tables involved.

Example 5 *In our running example, T_id is the primary key attribute for table T. An attribute with the same name is also contained in table A and is actually meant to be a foreign key attribute. It constitutes a one-to-many relationship between T and A. For tables A and C, we observe a foreign key attribute C_id in table A, pointing to the primary key attribute, again with the same name, in table C. Here, we have a many-to-one relationship between A and C.*

Within this scenario, another important operator can be applied: the *join*. A join combines tuples from one or more relations, often based on the condition of the equality of primary key and foreign key attribute values, which is an example of a so-called *natural join*.

Conceptually, the Cartesian product of the two relations is formed, i.e. the concatenation of each tuple from the first relation with each tuple from the second relation. Then, from this new relation, those tuples are selected that obey the equality restriction.

In practice, the expensive computation of the Cartesian product is not executed. Rather, special data structures such as indexes are used for a fast computation of joins. *Indexes* can be used to quickly find rows in a table given values for a certain attribute, e.g. a primary key value.

Further, there are special joins that are often applied in RDB systems, so-called *outer joins*. It may be the case that for a tuple in one of two relations to be joined there is none in the other relation with a corresponding key attribute value. With a natural inner join, the tuple from the first relation would be lost. With an outer join, the resulting relation contains the tuple from the first relation, extended with an appropriate number of missing values or NULL values in place of attribute values for a tuple from the second relation. Examples for joins can be found in later chapters.

2.2.2   Normal Forms and Universal Relations

One of the reasons for multi-relational data representation — besides the obvious idea to represent different kinds of objects with the help of different tables — is the desirabilty of compactness, especially the avoidance of redundancies, and with the latter the avoidance of so-called update anomalies.

Since KDD conventionally analyses only snapshots of databases, updates are not in the primary focus here. However, when dealing with data mining in relational databases, the methods for the design of databases are of interest. Here, this is especially normalization. Relations can be in a normal form at different levels.

For instance, for a first normal form, components of the tuples constituting a relation must not be any structured values such as `list` or `set` but just values of atomic types such as `integer` or `character`. For the second and third normal forms, certain dependencies of attributes within one relation are in focus. The elimination of those dependencies leads usually to a larger number of smaller tables. We do not go into details of these processes here but point to a so-called fourth normal form [41], which is of special relevance for our purposes.

Example 6 *Heuer and colleagues [41, pp. 82–83] provide the following example, cf. Figure 2.4. The depicted relation means that a person can have a set of children and a set of toys. These two sets are independent of each other. In other words, each child may play with each toy.*

Note that a table such as this one would not be an appropriate target table for conventional KDD, at least not for learning models concerning entities such as James Bond, since those entities are obviously described by more than one row here.

ACT		
Name	Child	Toy
James Bond	Hugo	Skyscraper
James Bond	Egon	Skyscraper
James Bond	Hugo	Rainbow Hopper
James Bond	Egon	Rainbow Hopper
James Bond	Hugo	AirCrusher
James Bond	Egon	AirCrusher

Figure 2.4: An example relation in third normal form

The given relation can be transformed to the situation depicted in Figure 2.5 with relations in fourth normal form. Note also that the natural join of those two relations produces the original one.

For KDD, another table would be necessary with one line to describe James Bond, with the Name attributes of the other tables as foreign key attributes pointing to the Name primary key attribute of that new table.

AC	
Name	Child
James Bond	Hugo
James Bond	Egon

AT	
Name	Toy
James Bond	Skyscraper
James Bond	Rainbow Hopper
James Bond	AirCrusher

Figure 2.5: Derived relations in fourth normal form

Exactly such a transformation from third normal form to fourth normal form was necessary for one of the data sets within our experiments, viz. those for KDD Cup 2001, cf. Appendix B. If not stated otherwise, we will assume relations in fourth normal form in the following.

There was also research in the database area aiming at simpler than the multi-relational situation. The motivation was to achieve simpler query languages, without the necessity of join operations. Here, ideas of *universal relations* were developed, and multiple methods to generate them [40, pp. 319–321]. Basically, a UR can be imagined as a join of the relations in an originally normalized multi-relational database. We return to the issue of URs in Chapter 5.

2.2.3   Further Relevant Issues

In the following chapters, we often use *graphs induced by relational databases*, in the sense of graph theory. Here, a vertex or node of the graph is constructed for each relation from the database, while edges can represent foreign key relationships. In this case, edges conventionally point from the foreign key attribute of a relation to the primary key attribute of another relation. This way, we arrive at a directed graph. An example is provided with our running example, cf. Appendix D. Further, we occasionally use undirected graphs, where edges do not have a direction.

Another prominent feature of relational database systems beyond the initial definitions of relational algebra [1] is the application of aggregate functions. Cabibbo and Torlone [21] note that beyond the *de facto* standard provided with SQL, which includes functions for the computation of averages, counts, maxima, minima, and sums, there are gaps in the common understanding and basic theoretical work in this area.

However, there are also a number of proposals even for user-defined aggregates and their implementation / application, e.g. by Wang and Zaniolo [131]. Since aggregate functions play a crucial role in this thesis, we will return to the subject later in this chapter.

For a finish of this section, we point to ideas arising out of the database area, which can be counted to the evolving research domain of multi-relational data mining (MRDM). For instance, Sattler and Dunemann suggest database primitives for more efficiently learning decision trees from databases [116]. Shang and colleagues propose methods for efficient frequent pattern mining in relational databases [119], which is of central relevance for association rule discovery in these environments. In general, MRDM has a strong relationship to the domain of Inductive Logic Programming (ILP), which is the topic of the following section.

2.3 Inductive Logic Programming

The means of ILP further increase expressive power, compared to RDB. Moreover, it was historically the first and for several years the only area of science to deal with learning from multi-relational data. ILP can be seen as the intersection of machine learning and logic programming [76].

Central ideas from machine learning are the basis for KDD. Relevant issues were briefly presented above, cf. Section 2.1. This section provides an overview of the basics of logics and logic programming as needed for this thesis. After that we turn to several ILP concepts and systems that we use in the following chapters. A good overview of ILP for KDD was provided by Wrobel [135].

2.3.1 Propositional Logic and Predicate Logic

For this section, we draw on material by Nienhuys-Cheng and Wolf [93] and Dassow [26]. Details should be looked up there, since we provide an overview only.

Logics help to formally describe (our models of) parts of the real world and are intended for automatic reasoning. For these purposes, *syntax* definitions have to be provided to state which strings form expressions or formulas allowed in a logical language. These expressions are usually finite.

Further, *semantics* have to be defined, in order to allow for truth values to be associated with those expressions, based on truth values of their atomic building blocks, w. r. t. some real-world situation.

For *reasoning*, inference operators can be defined, for instance, to syntactically derive certain expressions from others in a way that semantic statements can be made about the results.

Many relevant concepts in logics can be more easily explained for the case of propositional logic and then carried over to predicate logic. We attempt to do this in the following.

Propositional Logic

Atomic building blocks or *atoms* for expressions in propositional logic are so-called propositional variables such as p and q. They are symbols for propositions, i. e. sentences e. g. in natural language such as: "The earth is smaller than the sun." Propositional variables are associated with truth values *true* or *false*, often coded as 1 and 0, respectively. Truth value assignments depend on the characteristics of the symbolized proposition.

Usually, recursive definitions are provided for the construction of more complex expressions from simpler expressions. Such a definition would allow for certain concatenations of propositional variables with symbols for the logical operators for negation $\neg$, conjunction $\wedge$, disjunction $\vee$ and possibly more; further parantheses or other means to clarify the order of the application of operators.

Given truth values for propositional variables, those for more complex expressions can be assigned truth values using so-called truth tables, which provide results for the logical operators for basic cases. An example is the negation of a propositional variable, which is *true* iff the variable is associated with value *false*. Another example is the disjunction of two propositional variables, which is *true* iff at least one of the propositional variables is *true*.

A *literal* is an atom with or without a preceding symbol for negation.

A central concept is that of *logical consequence* or *logical entailment*: here, an expression A follows from another expression B iff A is true for all assignments of truth values to propositional variables that make B true. Since the number of propositional variables is finite in logical expressions, logical consequence relations can be investigated, e. g. by using truth tables again. However, these tables have a size exponential in the number of propositional variables involved.

An interesting point to note is that for any expression, there are expressions with the same semantics in special forms, so-called normal forms, e. g. conjunctive normal form (CNF). In a CNF expression, literals occur in disjunctions, which are in turn combined in conjunctions. Normal forms can be constructed algorithmically from any expression.

Often, expressions in CNF are written as *clause sets*, with disjunctions as the basis for clauses. For instance, $((p \vee q) \wedge (\neg p \vee \neg q))$ could be rewritten as a clause set $\{\{p, q\}, \{\neg p, \neg q\}\}$.

Clause sets form the basis for inference methods such as *resolution*. Resolution can also answer questions about logical consequence. For efficient resolution, subsets of possible clause sets have turned out to be favorable, especially *Horn clauses*, where a Horn clause contains at most one non-negated propositional variable.

Clauses can also be written as implications. Often, $\rightarrow$ is used as a symbol for implication. Then, $(\neg p \vee q)$ and $(p \rightarrow q)$ have the same values for the same assignments of truth values to the propositional variables. This is a case of *semantical equivalence*.

In logic programming, implications are often written with the symbol $\leftarrow$ in scientific texts and the symbol :- in code. To the left of those symbols, we find the so-called *head* of the implication. To the right, there is the so-called *body*.

Note that $(p \vee \neg q)$ and $(p \leftarrow q)$ are semantically equivalent. Further we remind the reader of DeMorgan's rule that $\neg(\neg p \vee \neg q)$ is semantically equivalent to $(p \wedge q)$. These issues provide some background for the following considerations.

For Horn clauses, there are three cases.

1. The Horn clause consists of a single positive literal, e. g. $\{p\}$. This can be written as $p \leftarrow$, also without the arrow. This construct is called a Horn fact.

2. The Horn clause consists of a positive literal and a number of negative literals, e. g. $\{p, \neg q_1, ..., \neg q_n\}$. This can be written as $p \leftarrow q_1 \wedge ... \wedge q_n$. This construct is called a Horn rule.

3. The Horn clause consists of a number of negative literals, e. g. $\{\neg q_1, ..., \neg q_n\}$. This can be written as $\leftarrow q_1 \wedge ... \wedge q_n$. This construct is called a Horn query.

The expressive power of propositional logics is rather restricted. For example, if two propositions symbolized by p and q are related, e. g. "The earth is smaller than the sun." and "The earth is larger than the moon.", there are no means within propositional logic to make this relationship explicit and to exploit it for reasoning. Similarly, a proposition such as "All planets in our system are smaller than the sun." would pose difficulties for propositional logic.

Predicate Logic

Predicate logic or *first-order logic* can help in cases as mentioned above, although at the cost of larger complexity. Expressions are built here from atomic building blocks again, which are relation or *predicate* symbols that take a certain number of arguments in parantheses, e. g. *smaller(earth, sun)* or *smaller(moon, earth)*. The number of arguments is called *arity* of a predicate. Atoms are *true* or *false* w. r. t. corresponding models of the real world. Interestingly, propositional variables can be seen as predicate symbols with zero arguments.

The arguments of predicates are *terms*. Terms can be *constants*, which are symbols for some real-world object, e. g. *earth* in the example above. Terms can also be *function* symbols, again with a certain number of arguments in parantheses. Arguments of functions are terms as well. An example is *satellite(earth)* to mean the *moon* or rather the object symbolized by that constant. Another kind of terms are *variables* such as X in *smaller(X, moon)*. Variables can be associated with real-world objects.

We adopt further conventions from logic programming here, where variable names are usually written with capital letters at the beginning, other names starting with lower case letters.

The *atoms* of predicate logic expressions — predicate symbols with the corresponding number of arguments — can again be connected by logical operators in the same way as in propositional logic. In addition, quantifiers for variables are possible: $\forall$ for universal quantification and $\exists$ for existential quantification. For instance, it is possible now to have an expression in a predicate logic such as $\forall X (planet(X) \rightarrow smaller(X, sun))$ which is supposed to mean that for all objects that are planets in our solar system it holds that they are smaller than the sun.

Logical consequence is not decidable in predicate logic. However, we can again compute normal forms and thus clause sets for predicate logic expressions. Then, we can apply resolution to finally arrive at statements about logical consequence

relations in a number of cases. Here, relevant concepts are substitution and
unification.

A *substitution* σ replaces all occurrences of a variable in an expression with
a term. For instance, an expression $p(X)$ can be subject to a substitution $\sigma =$
$\{X/a\}$ with p a predicate symbol, X a variable and a a constant, which would
result in an expression $p(a)$.

A *unification* attempts to make two expressions syntactically the same by
appropriately choosing substitutions. For instance, two expressions $p(X)$ and
$p(Y)$ can be unified with the help of a substitution such as $\sigma = \{X/a, Y/a\}$.

Prolog

To finish this part, we hint at Prolog [23] which stands for a programming language and automatic reasoning environment in the spirit of predicate logic. Here,
it is possible to express recursive structures in an elegant way, contrary to RDB
query languages. This power is exemplified here with the well-known predicate
definition for list membership.

```
member(X, [X|_]).
member(X, [_|Y]) :- member(X, Y).
```

We see two Prolog expressions in this example. Dots at their end are a
syntactic specialty of Prolog. Lists are enclosed by brackets in Prolog, and |
separates the list's head, i. e. the first element of the list, from the list's rest,
the so-called tail. X and Y are implicitly universally quantified variables here,
with X standing for an element of a list and Y for a list. The first expression is a
so-called fact, the second a so-called rule, cf. their variants in propositional logic
explained above.

The first expression means that an object is an element of a list, if it is to be
found at the head of the list. If not, the second expression comes into play and
means that an element is a member of a list if it can be found in the list's tail,
which has to be checked by recursively calling the Prolog program made up of the
two expressions again, now with the tail of the original list as second argument.

For instance, if we would like to find out if b is an element of the list [a,b,c],
a query ?-member(b, [a,b,c]). can be asked to the Prolog system. For the first
expression of the above Prolog program, there is no substitution possible, while for
the second, there can be the following substitution applied $\sigma = \{X/a, Y/[b, c]\}$.
So, the query resulting from the body of the rule, i. e. member(X, Y), for a
recursive call would now be ?-member(b, [b,c]). Here, a substitution $\sigma =$
$\{X/b\}$ can be found that makes the first expression succeed. Thus, the system
delivers a positive answer to our original question.

In the following, we often use special subsets of Prolog expressions. Among
these are *function-free* expressions. Since constants can be regarded as func-

tions with zero arguments, there can be only variables in argument positions of predicates here.

Further, we regularly use *ground facts* which correspond to atoms with no variables in argument positions. Also, we frequently use *non-structured facts* which means that only constants and variables are allowed as arguments. Together, ground and non-structured facts are atoms with constants in all argument positions. Note the correspondence of the arguments of those facts to tuples in relations of relational databases, and the correspondence of predicate symbols to relation names.

2.3.2 Basic Concepts of Inductive Logic Programming

ILP algorithms aim at learning logic programs, i.e. essentially clause sets, often restricted to Prolog style, from examples that are also represented as logic programs. For instance, from positive examples such as member(b, [a,b,c]). and negative examples such as :- member(d, [a,b,c]). the recursive definition of member/2 (2 means that the membership predicate takes two arguments here, i.e. the arity of the member predicate) as given in the preceding section should be learned.

Often, ILP learning tasks thus involve to get from an extensional definition of a so-called target predicate to a more compact intensional definition; in other words, from examples in the form of ground facts to non-ground rules. These rules should then be applicable to unseen examples, for instance, in order to classify them as positive or negative, i.e. belonging to the target concept or not.

Background Knowledge

A distinctive feature of ILP is the usage of *background knowledge* beside the examples. For instance, the member/2 predicate definition might also be provided as *input* for learning of other predicates that model aspects of working with lists. Actually, there are different views on background knowledge to be found in the ILP literature.

Often, all predicate definitions except that for the target predicate are considered to be background knowledge [135]. Occasionally, however, only items that exist independently of the specific learning examples are regarded as background knowledge [108]. Here, "independent" means that the corresponding piece of knowledge is not of concern for one example only, as information about exclusive parts of the example would be, for instance. An example is provided with the original representation of the KRK.illegal learning task, cf. Appendix B.

We adopt to the first view of background knowledge. Further, we take the perspective that ILP methods in a wider sense can include those that learn from multi-relational representations but do not necessarily arrive at knowlege represented in the form of logic programs.

Bias

If the aim is learning logic programs, the hypothesis spaces are usually huge. In order to successfully search here, an appropriate *bias* is necessary. Bias may concern the language used as well as search itself. Nedellec and colleagues [92] further distinguish validation bias from those named before, which is responsible for decisions about when to stop search. We also find other categorizations in the literature, e.g. syntactic bias vs. semantic bias [91]. All the authors agree, however, that it is useful to make bias as explicit as possible, arriving at a declarative bias, which is easy to manipulate by the user and even a basis for reasoning about and changing of the bias used in a certain learning situation.

We already introduced a kind of *language bias* with Horn clauses, which are the basis for Prolog's facts, rules, and queries.

In Prolog rule bodies, negation is allowed, which is why we deal with *program clauses* here.

Definition 4 *If argument positions for atoms are typed, we arrive at* deductive database (DDB) clauses. *Typing means that for each argument position, an information is provided which set of values can be associated with those arguments. Note the resemblance to relational databases in this respect.*

Definition 5 *Further restrictions can be put on those clauses to arrive at* deductive hierarchical database (DHDB) clauses, *where recursive structures in both predicate and type definitions are not allowed.*

Other types of clauses that are frequently used in ILP are the following.

Definition 6 *A clause is a* constrained clause *iff all body variables also occur in the head of the rule.*

Definition 7 Determinate clauses *have determinate body literals. A literal is determinate iff all "new" variables have a unique binding given the bindings of all the other, the "old" variables. Old variables occur earlier in the clause, i.e. to the left of the literal in focus. Prolog will have found bindings for those old variables when it comes to considering the current literal.*

Binding a variable means here especially substitution with a constant. Thus, determinacy of a literal is given iff there is either (a) exactly one substitution for new variables such that the literal can be derived by the Prolog program given, or (b) no such substitution.

Case (b) is often not emphasized in the literature, but see Nienhuys-Cheng and Wolf [93, p. 335]. Restricting the definition to case (a) would mean that information might be lost, similar to a situation with missing outer joins in relational databases. For further processing, a special constant "?" is often used in ILP systems to indicate an equivalent for the NULL value in RDBs.

Example 7 *Given two target examples described by Prolog ground and unstructured facts:* p(1,a). *and* p(2,b)., *further a single background knowledge fact, also ground and unstructured:* q(2,c). *The Prolog clause* p(X,Y) :- q(X,Z). *is determinate according to our definition, although there is no* q *literal for the first example in the background knowledge.*

With a definition restricted to case (a), the clause would not be considered determinate, and predicate q *would be neglected for learning by corresponding systems.*

If a body literal uses variables from the head only, apart from new variables, those new variables are defined to have *depth* 1. If a body literal uses old variables with maximum depth n and introduces new variables, the latter have depth $n+1$. A clause is an *i-determinate clause* if there occur variables in the clause of depth at most i.

Definition 8 *A clause is a* linked clause *iff there is at least one old variable among the arguments of each body literal.*

Further kinds of language bias, which are often applied, are restrictions to function-free hypothesis languages and to ground facts for examples, often for background knowledge as well. There were also methods proposed to transform non-ground knowledge into ground facts, cf. hints given by Lavrač and Flach [77]. The same authors provide examples for further simple kinds of language bias, e. g. by restricting the number of literals in clauses, or the number of variables.

Considering *search bias*, there are many approaches to constructing logic programs from examples. For instance, in a top-down approach, rules are built by successively adding literals. The choice of those literals may be made w. r. t. certain criteria such as information gain, cf. Section 2.1.

Usually, there is a trade-off to be made here. With a very strict bias, efficiency of learning will be high, but the hypothesis searched for may not be in the chosen language or missed during search. With a more relaxed bias, more hypotheses are in the realms of search, which may then take much longer, though.

Subsumption and Coverage

Further basic concepts in ILP are those of subsumption and coverage.

Subsumption, also called θ-subsumption, refers to a relation between clauses. For two clauses C and D, C subsumes D if there exists a substitution θ such that $C\theta \subseteq D$, i. e. every literal in $C\theta$ is also in D. A part of the relevance of subsumption is expressed in the subsumption theorem, cf. details provided by Nienhuys-Cheng and Wolf [93], which states important relationships with logical consequence. Subsumption will also play a role within our approach as presented in the following chapters.

Coverage means the following here. Given a first-order hypothesis containing rules and ground background knowledge B. Then, a ground example e is said to be covered by the hypothesis, if it contains a rule $T \leftarrow Q$ with $T\theta = e$ and $Q\theta \subseteq B$. This is called extensional coverage by Lavrač and Džeroski [76].

2.3.3   Prominent Systems for ILP

In this part of the thesis, we give short overviews of three systems for ILP, viz. FOIL, PROGOL, and TILDE, which belong to the most frequently used from a large number of ILP systems that were introduced within the last 15 years. All three systems belong to the group of those that search first-order hypothesis spaces and come up with corresponding models. Also, they are all top-down learning systems, i.e. they start learning with a most general hypothesis covering all examples, which is specialized afterwards with the help of a *refinement operator* [120] to build a new clause D from a given clause C with $C\theta \subseteq D$.

However, there are also essential differences between the systems, which make the consideration of all three seem worthwhile. For instance, FOIL uses a covering approach to rule learning, PROGOL applies an especially guided A*-like search, and TILDE upgrades decision tree learning methods to the case of first-order logic. All three systems are used for our empirical work as presented later in this thesis.

FOIL

FOIL was first presented by Quinlan in 1990 [103], further advances in 1993 and 1995 [105, 106]. It combines ideas from ILP with approaches from propositional machine learning.

From ILP, it inherits the usage of clauses with their expressive power up to learning recursive hypotheses. Positive and negative examples E represent the target relation. Background knowledge B consists of some other relations. E and B have the form of tuples of constants and present the input for FOIL, together with schema information.

From propositional machine learning, the system uses typical approaches for constructing hypotheses built of rules and approaches for the evaluation of parts of hypotheses.

Basically, FOIL consists of two main loops, an outer loop and an inner loop, as typical for the covering algorithm for learning of rules [82]. The outer loop is running while there are still positive examples left in the training set, initially E. An inner loop is started to build a clause that characterizes a part of the target relation. Starting from a clause with an empty body, literals are added to the body to avoid the coverage of negative examples. Literal evaluation is achieved using criteria based on information theory again, cf. Section 2.1. If such a clause is found, all positive examples that are covered by the clause are removed from the training set.

We do not go into further detail here, but just mention that FOIL also uses strategies for overcoming myopia — a single literal may be of not much value when considered for introduction on its own, but of high value in combination with others — and for avoiding problems with infinite recursion. Moreover, pruning strategies are applied and inexact definitions are allowed.

Quinlan states at the end of his early FOIL paper [103] that the system will be adequate for handling learning tasks of practical significance, in the context of relational databases, partly caused by the correspondence of FOIL's input format with the format of relational databases. Our experimental results provide support for Quinlan's prediction.

PROGOL

PROGOL was presented by Muggleton in 1995 [88] as a system that implements inverse entailment. Muggleton and Firth also provided a good tutorial introduction to the system [90].

The input for Progol consists of examples and background knowledge, where especially the latter may include non-ground and structured rules. Furthermore, mode declarations have to be provided by the user, declaring among others the target predicate, types of arguments, places for old or new variables or constants.

For each example, Progol constructs a most specific clause within the mode language that is implied by the mode declarations.

For our purposes, i.e. in our experiments with all relations represented by ground non-structured facts, a most specific clause has the target predicate literal corresponding to the learning example in focus as head, and a conjunction of all facts to be found in the background knowledge which are related to the learning example as body.

These most specific clauses are then used to guide an A*-like search [94] through the clauses which subsume the most specific clauses.

TILDE

TILDE was presented by Blockeel and DeRaedt in 1998 [14] and has been further developed since then. It is now a part of the ACE system, cf. Appendix A.

TILDE is an upgrade of Quinlan's C4.5 [104] and reuses many of the methods of propositional decision tree learning as sketched above, cf. Section 2.1. It uses the same heuristics as C4.5, among others *gain ratio* for the decision about questions to ask in nodes. Gain ratio is derived from information gain but does not have the same unjustified preference for attributes with many distinct values. TILDE also applies pruning mechanisms as C4.5.

Differences to the propositional case are that nodes contain a conjunction of literals and different nodes may share variables, with certain restrictions. The set of tests at a node is computed with the help of a refinement operator under

θ-subsumption. This operator is specified by the user with the help of mode declarations similar to those as used by PROGOL.

The system includes special features for lookahead to overcome myopia of search, for discretization, and many more, e.g. for dealing with large data sets.

The authors [14] further state that first-order decision trees show higher expressive power than flat normal logic programs as induced by many other ILP systems such as TILDE and PROGOL.

Summary

ILP systems show remarkable abilities, e.g. for learning recursive theories from few and complex examples. However, they tend to be inefficient for learning from larger sets of data as in real-life business databases. Further, high efforts may be necessary to run them appropriately, for instance for producing declaration files or for setting intricate parameters. We return to these issues in Chapter 4.

2.4 Preparation for Knowledge Discovery

Although data preparation causes the largest part of costs within KDD projects, research has mainly focused on the more central step of KDD, viz. data mining algorithms. The need for data preparation, though, is well-known and already led to many tools. These are also included in commercial environments for KDD, to be applied by knowledgeable data analysts.

As Pyle puts it [101], the task of data preparation for data mining is twofold: the data have to be transformed such that data mining algorithms can be applied with high prospects for success, and the analyst has to become informed for mining and for the evaluation and application of the results.

In a multi-relational scenario, e.g. with data from a relational database to be analyzed, a number of proposals and systems were provided to help the analyst. Among them are suggestions for combining and modifying data sets [114], ultimatly by the user with the help of database query languages.

Systems such as MININGMART [30, 87] or XELOPES [125] further support the user in multi-relational data preparation with means for the easy application of operators, up to opportunities to archive successful data preprocessing procedures for later access in similar projects. There is also a tendency towards the usage of standardized languages such as the Predictive Model Markup Language (PMML).

In the following, we focus on aspects of data preparation that are of special relevance for the following chapters.

2.4.1 Feature Construction

For KDD with a single table input for the data mining algorithm, feature construction means the creation of new columns for that single table.

Algorithms for conventional feature construction have also a single table input and compute new attributes from one or more of the attributes given in that table. For instance, from two attributes that describe the length and width of an object, its area may be computed.

In a broader sense, manipulations of single existing attributes can also be allocated in the realms of conventional feature construction.

An example would be discretization, where a numeric attribute could be replaced by a nominal attribute that symbolizes ranges of the former numeric values with the help of names.

Another example would be range normalization, e. g. by dividing the length values of all target objects by their maximum in order to arrive at an attribute for length with values between 0 and 1.

A final example here would be a coding of nominal attributes with n possible values by n binary attributes that indicate the occurrence of the possible nominal values.

Propositionalization is also an approach for feature construction. However, an algorithm for propositionalization takes multiple relations as input and usually concerns more complex structures than conventional feature construction. Here, new attributes are computed from specifics of several objects related to a target object. More details can be found in the following chapters.

2.4.2 Feature Selection

Considering again the conventional case of data mining with a single table input, it is usually good to have a larger number of rows in such a table. With a growing number of learning examples as represented by those rows, the statistics and heuristics that form the basis for learning get more reliable, as a rule.

The situation is different w. r. t. the number of columns, though. Here, larger numbers mean growing hypothesis spaces, which not only endanger efficiency of search but also effectivity, e. g. when dangers to arrive at only locally optimal solutions grow, or other dangers of overfitting.

Perhaps even more contra-intuitive are findings such as the following. For classification tasks, not only features without a correlation with the target attribute can have negative effects for learning, but also features with certain predictive potentials as demonstrated by John [51], among others. Approaches to feature (subset) selection can improve the situation, for an overview see the book by Liu and Motoda [79].

Feature selection methods are often classified into *filters* and *wrappers* [79, 132]. While filters choose attributes based on general properties of the data before learning takes place, wrappers intermingle feature selection and learning. The methods for feature selection are also often subdivided into those that judge only single attributes at a time and those that evaluate and compare whole sets of attributes. The former are also called univariate methods, the latter multivariate methods. Furthermore, different selection criteria and search strategies can be applied.

Approaches to dimensionality reduction have also been developed within ILP, e.g. by Alphonse and Matwin [3]. Especially in the context of propositionaliza- tion, where unsupervised feature construction may lead to many redundant or otherwise irrelevant attributes, a selection of the good features seems advisable. It was in fact investigated on several occasions e.g. by Lavrač and Flach [77] and by ourselves [72, 73], see Chapter 5.

2.4.3 Aggregation

Cabibbo and Torlone [21] state that aggregate functions have always been consid- ered an important feature of practical database query languages, but a systematic study of those has evolved only slowly. In many cases, the aggregate functions as provided by SQL were in the focus of the investigations. In fact, the same holds for large parts of our investigations as presented in this thesis.

The authors [21] let $\{\{\mathcal{N}\}\}$ denote the class of finite multisets of values from a countably infinite domain $\mathcal{N}$ and define an *aggregate function* over $\mathcal{N}$ as a total function from $\{\{\mathcal{N}\}\}$ to $\mathcal{N}$, mapping each multiset of values to a value. Our view largely corresponds to that definition, although $\mathcal{N}$ may be a finite set, and the function values may also come from a set of values different from $\mathcal{N}$, for instance when counting a certain value of a nominal attribute.

Aggregate functions are often used in statistics to describe properties of sam- ples of populations, e.g. averages or standard deviations. Categories of such mea- sures are described by Fahrmeir and colleagues [31] or Hand and colleagues [38], among others. Properties of aggregate operators are investigated by Detyniecky [29]. We focus for our work on aggregate functions with close relationships to SQL as mentioned above, but also on computational complexity, as investigated by Körnig [57] and further discussed in Chapter 5.

Aggregate functions are widely applied within KDD and related areas, as exemplified in the following. During data preparation, analysts often investigate statistical properties such as histograms of nominal attributes, in order to make decisions about which attributes to use, for instance.

Outlier detection and missing value replacement often rely on aggregate func- tions as well. Tools for these steps of data preparation can be found in many KDD environments. Aggregate functions may also be used to integrate [117] or compress [45] data.

Last not least, domain experts often apply aggregate functions when manu- ally transforming multi-relational data into inputs for conventional data mining systems.

In *data warehousing* and *online analytical processing* (OLAP), aggregate func- tions are also typical. Here, users investigate large volumes of data by the interac- tive use of special operators for navigation, which often involve the computation of sums and averages. For efficiency reasons, aggregate function values may also be pre-computed here. Overviews are given by Inmon and colleagues [47] and Bauer and colleagues [6], while Gray and colleagues [36] discuss the central data cube operator.

For our purposes, we focus on a special kind of application of aggregate functions with two relevant aspects.

First, we investigate the automatic application of aggregate functions to multisets of values of an attribute shared by several objects, which are related to a target object in the focus of learning. This should be distinguished from usual applications of aggregate functions in KDD systems, e. g. when an average of a numeric attribute is computed across all target objects.

Second, the results of aggregation are supposed to be used as input for conventional data mining, i. e. automatic methods for knowledge discovery. This should be distinguished from what is typical for OLAP systems, where it is the user's task to exploit the results of aggregate functions.

2.5 Summary

In this chapter, we reviewed issues from the areas of conventional knowledge discovery in databases, relational databases, and inductive logic programming. This order reflects the increasing expressive power of the typical means of knowledge representation in the areas: starting from single tables and propositional models in KDD, via multiple relations in RDB, to the means of first-order logic in ILP. Finally, we focused on aspects of data preparation for data mining, where propositionalization as detailed in the following chapter can be allocated.

Chapter 3

A General Model for Propositionalization

In this chapter, we present a formal framework for propositionalization. We then describe prominent traditional approaches to propositionalization with the means of our framework.

In preparation, we state our demands concerning such a framework and define our notion of propositionalization. We also point to advantages and disadvantages of propositionalization.

As early as the concept of propositionalization was formed [58, 60], there was already a number of approaches following its general idea. However, a general theory for propositionalization or a formalization of the basics of those approaches was missing. In the following, we provide such a formalization, with the following objectives:

- The framework should provide opportunities for a precise description of the essentials of existing approaches to propositionalization.

- The framework should provide opportunities to unify the various descriptions from the literature and thus allow for an easier understanding, evaluation, and comparison of the approaches.

- The framework should provide opportunities to enhance existing approaches with new means for propositionalization. Also, the framework should facilitate combinations of components of different approaches.

We will return to these criteria for our framework in the appropriate places later in this thesis.

A number of views on propositionalization can be found in the literature. They vary in the points what the object of transformations is or if conventional propositional learning is a part of propositionalization, among others. We define our notion of propositionalization here.

Definition 9 Propositionalization *is the process of transforming a relational representation of data and background knowledge into the format of a single table that can serve as the input to a propositional learning system.*

More precise information about inputs and outputs for propositionalization and about the transformation of the inputs into the outputs follow in the next section.

Demands we have to put on an approach to propositionalization are first of all that for

- effectiveness

- efficiency

- ease of use

By *effectiveness*, we mean the quality of learning results, e. g. validation error rates for learned classifiers. A positive effect would be that such an estimate is significantly lower than those of competing systems.

Efficiency first of all means the time it takes to arrive at the learning results. In KDD practice, we assume that those times should not exceed a range of several hours. Of course, less time consumption would be positive. We also compare efficiency of different approaches.

The criterion of *ease of use* is more difficult to measure. We do not go beyond rather general considerations here. We consider essential steps that the user must take to run the different systems, especially including efforts for a further preparation of the data and for setting parameters.

We call these three points of effectiveness, efficiency, and ease of use the 3E criteria. We will consider these properties in this and the following chapters.

De Raedt [107] showed that propositionalization produces an explosive number of features, if information from the original multi-relational representation of data is to be preserved completely, i. e. without information loss, in the general case. Here, *information loss* means that the original data cannot be recovered from results of propositionalization. However, acceptance of a certain information loss caused by heuristic restrictions to propositionalization led to many interesting results.

As a further motivation for the consideration of propositionalization, we see the following points. The result of propositionalization can be the input to a wide spectrum of data mining systems, according to the preferences of the user or to availability. Those conventional data mining systems often show high efficiency as well.

Moreover, a data mining system can easily be used with different parameterizations on a propositionalization result. This is suggested by KDD process models with the loops contained therein. Such loops are often useful according to the experience of the author as well. Experience was gathered during the CoIL Challenge 2000 [63], KDD Cups 2001, 2002 and 2003 [22, 64, 68, 69, 70], Data Mining Cups 2002 and 2003 [66] and SAS Mining Challenges 2002 and 2003 [65, 44, 42, 43].

In ILP [77], advantages of propositionalization over traditional approaches are identified in a more flexible usage of negation, and the opportunity to build libraries of constructed features for similar types of tasks. The main drawback of propositionalization is seen here in the inability to learn recursive clauses.

Further disadvantages of the approach can be seen in the extra efforts that are necessary for managing the results of propositionalization, although it can be also an advantage to have a well-organized archive of data sets for data mining.

Another, more basic problem of the approach is that of information loss during the transformation process. This can be at least theoretically so severe that effectivity cannot be guaranteed. Nevertheless, we will show empirically that competitive results can be reached despite the problem of information loss.

Still, it might offer a higher flexibility to learn directly from relational data as originally intended by traditional ILP systems. For these reasons, we include applications of such systems into our experiments.

3.1   A Framework for Propositionalization

In this section, ideas from our earlier work [71] are further developed into a framework for propositionalization to accommodate the traditional approaches and their follow-up systems.

As usual in ILP, we assume here that we are given a set of positive examples E^+, a set of negative examples E^-, and background knowledge B. Since we are mainly dealing with data originating in relational databases, we will assume that E^+ is a set of ground p-atoms, i. e., atoms the predicate of which is the target predicate p (of arity a). Similarly, E^- is a set of ground negated p-atoms, and B is a set of ground atoms using different background knowledge predicates.

Of course, there can be sources of data and knowledge different from relational databases. In the more general case of logic programming, there could thus arise structured facts, possibly non-ground, and rules as well. For these cases, methods such as flattening were proposed before, e. g. sketched by Lavrač and Flach [77], or for finding h-easy ground models [89].

Although these methods form a first occasion for the loss of information, we transform other kinds of representations of examples and background knowledge into ground facts before propositionalization. This provides a unified starting point and we will further exemplify the usefulness of this step later on in the sections on our empirical work.

The learning task can now be adopted from Definition 3. There, E is a set of tuples or feature vectors. Here, E^+ and E^- are sets of first-order atoms. So we use E with a slight difference here, by defining $E = E^+ \cup E^-$. Differences in meaning such as this one should be clarified by the context of the usage of our nomenclature. In addition to E, background knowledge B can now be used for learning. Thus, Definition 3 is adopted to

- **Given:** E^+, E^-, B as described above.

- **Find:** A hypothesis h from a set of allowed hypotheses L such that the error of h on future instances is minimized.

Since all examples show the same predicate symbol, we also call this learning task the *single-predicate learning task*.[1] Actually, we are ultimately not restricted to concept or classifier learning but could also easily adopt to clustering tasks, for instance, as will be shown later in this section.

In ILP, h is usually a set of first-order clauses, and a new instance is classified as positive if and only if it is covered by this set of clauses. In a *transformation-based* approach to ILP, on the other hand, we assume we are given a transformation function τ which transforms the given E^+, E^-, and B into a single propositional table. One then uses a propositional learner on this table, producing a propositional hypothesis h which can then be used to classify future instances, which of course first need to be transformed by τ as well.

Depending on the transformation and the propositional learner that are used, in certain cases it is even possible to transform the propositional learning results back into an equivalent clausal theory [75, 76]. Here, a restriction applies concerning propositional learners. Their results must have the form of rules or — as in the case of trees — it must be possible to convert the propositional learning results into rules. Conventional support vector machines, for instance, cannot be used since their results cannot be converted into first-order rules in a straightforward way.

In principle, designers of transformation-based ILP systems are not restricted to any particular form of τ functions. In practice, it is commonplace to base the transformation on an implicit first-order hypothesis space L, and use the literals and variable bindings of the clauses in L to define the transformation.

For example, in the pioneering work on LINUS [75], a space of constrained clauses was used, whereas in its successor system DINUS [76], a space of determinate clauses [89] was used instead. As an alternative, if selected arbitrary clauses are used, one can apply existential transformations and use the clauses as binary features [61, 77].

---

[1]Note that the information about examples being positive or negative can be contained in an extra argument of example atoms, rather than expressed by their membership to E^+ or E^-. In relational databases, the situation with extra arguments seems more common. Such extra arguments can also contain more than two class labels, or even numeric values.

In order to better understand the framework, and to allow for an easier description of our own work, we will now describe this process of defining transformation functions in more detail.

We will start by assuming that we are given a set $\mathcal{C}$ of clauses upon which
feature generation is to be based. Note that $\mathcal{C}$ can be a systematically defined
entire hypothesis space, but could also consist of a few selected clauses, so the
following formalization also covers the case of using individual clauses, perhaps
learned by a non-transformation-based ILP learner. As a piece of notation, for a
target predicate p of arity a, let

$$\top := p(X_1, ..., X_a) \tag{3.1}$$

denote the most general p-atom. Since we are considering a single predicate
learning task, we can assume without loss of generality that all $C \in \mathcal{C}$ have $\top$ as
head.

Let $vars(C)$ denote the ordered set of variables of C. For a clause C with

$$vars(C) = \{Y_1, ..., Y_m\} \tag{3.2}$$

and a ground p-atom e, let

$$val(C, e, B) := \{(Y_1\sigma, ..., Y_m\sigma) \mid C\sigma \subseteq B \cup \{e\}\} \tag{3.3}$$

denote the different value combinations assumed by the variables of C when
matching the clause head against the example and the clause body against the
background knowledge. For determinate clauses as described in Section 2.3,
$val(C, e, B)$ either contains exactly one tuple or is empty.

We can now define a propositionalization function φ as follows:

$$\varphi : C, val(C, e, B) \mapsto (v_1, ..., v_{n_{\varphi,C}}) \ . \tag{3.4}$$

In other words, φ produces the tuple of desired feature values for an example e
with respect to the literals and variable bindings of the clause C considering background knowledge B. C as first argument can be necessary in case $val(C, e, B)$
is the empty set, e. g. for producing a tuple of $n_{\varphi,C}$ symbols for missing values.

Sometimes, it will be useful to also have a function which generates not the
individual feature *values*, but the list of *names* (and *types*) of the features that
are the result of propositionalizing based on C:

$$\Phi : C \mapsto Att_1, ..., Att_{n_{\varphi,C}} \ . \tag{3.5}$$

In a propositional table, all examples must have the same attributes. For that
reason, Φ and the width of φ must not depend on e. Further, we assume that the
variables of each clause are typed, so φ and Φ can make use of this information
when performing the propositionalization.

The following example is the transformation used by Kramer [61] and Lavrač
and Flach [77] on selected (parts of) clauses to transform them into binary features.

Existential Features This transformation simply records *whether* C can be matched against the example e and background knowledge B:

$$\varphi_\exists(C, val(C, e, B)) := \left\{ \begin{array}{ll} (1) & \text{if } |\ val(C, e, B)\ | > 0 \ , \\ (0) & \text{otherwise.} \end{array} \right. \tag{3.6}$$

Counting Features As a slight generalization of the previous example, the following function counts *how often* C can be matched against the example e and background knowledge B:

$$\varphi_\#(C, val(C, e, B)) := (|\ val(C, e, B)\ |) \ . \tag{3.7}$$

In order to define the complete row of features corresponding to a particular example, we simply concatenate the features generated with respect to each clause in C with the values of the variables in $\top$. For a p-atom $e = \top\sigma$, the propositionalization with respect to C is defined as follows:

$$prop(C, e, B) := (X_1\sigma, ..., X_a\sigma) \bigoplus_{C \in \mathcal{C}} \varphi(C, val(C, e, B)) \ , \tag{3.8}$$

where $\oplus$ denotes tuple concatenation.

Finally, the propositionalized table of examples is defined as the union of all example propositionalizations, adding in the class attribute[2]:

$$\tau(\mathcal{C}, E^+, E^-, B) := \{prop(\mathcal{C}, e, B) \oplus (1) \mid e \in E^+\} \cup \{prop(\mathcal{C}, e, B) \oplus (0) \mid \neg e \in E^-\} \ . \tag{3.9}$$

Two remarks are in order here. First, the union operator should be applied only if all example descriptions are different, which would be the case if identifier values are included. Identifiers could also be produced by simply enumerating the examples. Otherwise, multisets should be used. Second, in the case of missing class information, e. g. for clustering tasks, the last step of adding a class attribute is omitted.

So far, background knowledge B was presented as consisting of non-target predicate definitions, as found in a relational database as non-target tables, for instance. This is not supposed to exclude the case where further predicates are introduced, e. g. special predicates such as =/2 or new relations as materialized views in a relational database. Such a further relation can even be produced by propositionalization as suggested above. This accommodates approaches such as those provided by Knobbe et al. [54]. However, we will show that this additional complexity should be integrated with care, see Chapter 4.

Our framework presents propositionalization as a process that leads from originally relational data to a single table representation of those data. In this

---

[2]Note that this definition can easily be adapted to the case where one of the arguments of $\top$ is the attribute to be predicted, cf. Footnote 1. Here, adding in the class attribute is simply left out, since class information is already contained in the corresponding argument.

section, we have focused on the central steps of propositionalization. In practice, specific pre-processing of the input and post-processing of the output of those central steps are useful. We will return to these issues in Chapter 5.

Here, we only mention that the original data should be first prepared such that the results for certain queries derived from clauses in $\mathcal{C}$ can be computed efficiently. Those query results have then to be condensed by some function φ and joined into a single table as achieved above by *prop* and τ. This single table may be further processed e.g. by special feature construction and feature subset selection methods to arrive at appropriate inputs for conventional KDD systems. Their output may finally be transformed back into relational knowledge such as first-order theories.

3.2   Traditional Approaches to Propositionalization

There are a number of existing approaches to propositionalization that apply heuristic restrictions to the process, thus allowing for a certain amount of information loss. Nevertheless, those approaches arrive in many cases at both theoretically and practically interesting results.

This section examines such methods. Going beyond the original presentations of the approaches, they are described here in a unified way within the framework presented above. We place a special focus on the pioneering systems LINUS and DINUS because they were especially influential for the area of research into propositionalization. They are also used in our empirical work.

3.2.1   LINUS

LINUS was first presented in detail by Lavrač [75] in 1990. It generalized ideas from Bratko and colleagues [18] that were applied for expert system design in a medical domain, especially the algorithm QuMAS (Qualitative Model Acquisition System). An introductory presentation of LINUS was provided by Lavrač and Džeroski in Section 5.4 of their book on ILP [76]. In the following, relevant parts of that presentation are adopted in the sense of our framework.

Examples in E^+ and E^- are ground facts and may contain structured, but non-recursive terms. As such, they are DHDB clauses, cf. Definition 5. The training examples provide an extensional definition of the target predicate p/a. The learning task is to find an intensional definition of this predicate that can be applied to unseen instances. Ultimately, this corresponds to the learning task as defined in our framework.

Background knowledge B can have the form of DDB clauses, cf. Definition 4. It may be non-ground, i.e. intensional, and possibly recursive. Furthermore, a symmetric predicate *equals* $=/2$ is a built-in predicate in LINUS and applicable to variables of the same type. It adds both expressivity and complexity. According to tasks described in the ILP book [76], background knowledge is frequently in the form of ground facts and non-structured. The same applies to examples. This form is also suggested as advantageous within our framework.

Clauses for the clause set $\mathcal{C}$ in the sense of our framework take the form

$$p(X_1, ..., X_a) : - < Atom > . \tag{3.10}$$

where $< Atom >$ can be one of the following

1. a positive constrained literal, cf. Definition 6, e.g. $q(X_i, X_j)$ or $X_i = X_j$ with $1 \leq i, j \leq a$, or

2. a positive determinate literal, cf. Definition 7, e.g. $r(X_i, X_j, Y)$ with $1 \leq i, j \leq a$ where Y has a unique binding given bindings of X_i and X_j.

Clause generation for $\mathcal{C}$ is typically exhaustive. That means, all possible applications of background predicates on the arguments of the target relation are computed, considering types. Each such possible application results in an attribute. For determinate body literals with more than one new variable, the corresponding number of new attributes is produced. Tuple construction is achieved by calling the corresponding predicates for each target relation tuple.

If a call of a constrained clause $C \in \mathcal{C}$ succeeds for an example, the corresponding feature value is set to *true*, else to *false*. This can be seen as an existential feature in the sense of the framework presented above. More elaborate, $val(C, e, B)$ contains at most one element, because of the usage of a constrained clause. With C and $val(C, e, B)$ as argument, $\varphi_\exists$ is applied as presented in our framework.

If a call of a determinate clause $C \in \mathcal{C}$ succeeds for an example, the corresponding feature value(s) is / are set to the values of the new variable(s) of the body literal. More elaborate, $val(C, e, B)$ contains at most one element, because of determinacy. The propositionalization function used here is identity φ_{id}, i.e. values of new variables in determinate literals are directly used as new attribute values.

After propositional rule or tree learning, learning results are converted back into a first-order theory. Clauses building the final LINUS theories have again $p(X_1, ..., X_a)$ as head. The body of a clause in a hypothesis is a conjunction of literals that can take the following forms.

1. a binding of a variable to a value, e.g. $X_i = x$ with $1 \leq i \leq a$,

2. an equality of pairs of variables occurring in the head of the clause, e.g. $X_i = X_j$ with $1 \leq i, j \leq a$,

3. a positive constrained literal, e.g. $q(X_i, X_j)$ with $1 \leq i, j \leq a$, and

4. a positive determinate literal and further literals to bind its new variables,
   e. g. $f(X_i, X_j, Y), Y = y$ with $1 \leq i, j \leq a$.

Thus, hypotheses take the form of constrained DHDB clauses. For (1) and numeric X, $X_i > x$ and $X_i < x$ are also allowed, analogous for (4) and numeric y. For guidance of induction by reducing the search space, any subset of the four cases can be excluded. For instance, focusing on (1) finally yields an attribute-value language, i. e. learning from the target relation only. So, the language bias in LINUS is declarative.

In the literature, there is often a restriction to (2) and (3), i. e. function-free clauses, which causes propositionalization results to be based on constrained clauses only, and hence such a table is completely Boolean.

Post-processing within LINUS especially involves irrelevant literal elimination. The treatment of irrelevancy is dealt with in this dissertation below.

We now illustrate with an example, which is adopted from Section 5.3.2 in the ILP book [76].

Example 8 *The target relation is* daughter(X,Y) *and means that person* X *is the daughter of person* Y. *The task is to define the target relation with the help of the background knowledge relations* female, male, *and* parent. *All variables are of type* $person = \{ann, eve, pat, sue, tom\}$. *Figure 3.1 shows the input data.*

Training examples		Background knowledge		
daughter(sue,eve).	pos	parent(eve,sue).	female(ann).	male(pat).
daughter(ann,pat).	pos	parent(ann,tom).	female(sue).	male(tom).
daughter(tom,ann).	neg	parent(pat,ann).	female(eve).	
daughter(eve,ann).	neg	parent(tom,sue).		

Figure 3.1: A *daughter* family relationship problem in Prolog form

$\mathcal{C}$ *contains the following clauses, here excluding* $=/2$:

1. *daughter(X,Y) :- female(X).*

2. *daughter(X,Y) :- female(Y).*

3. *daughter(X,Y) :- male(X).*

4. *daughter(X,Y) :- male(Y).*

5. *daughter(X,Y) :- parent(X,X).*

6. *daughter(X,Y) :- parent(X,Y).*

7. *daughter(X,Y) :- parent(Y,X).*

8. daughter(X,Y) :- parent(Y,Y).

Figure 3.2 shows the results of the application of the background knowledge predicates in the form of the clauses in C, with f for female, m for male, and p for parent.

Variables		Propositional features								
X	Y	f(X)	f(Y)	m(X)	m(Y)	p(X,X)	p(X,Y)	p(Y,X)	p(Y,Y)	class
sue	eve	1	1	0	0	0	0	1	0	pos
ann	pat	1	0	0	1	0	0	1	0	pos
tom	ann	0	1	1	0	0	0	1	0	neg
eve	ann	1	1	0	0	0	0	0	0	neg

Figure 3.2: Propositional form of the *daughter* relationship problem (1 for *true*, 0 for *false*)

Note that there are examples of redundant features given here, e. g. male because it is the complement of female, or parent(X,X) *because the set of its possible values is a singleton that cannot differentiate between positive and negative examples.*

From the propositional representation, an attribute value learner may induce a rule such as the following:

```
if [female(X) = 1] and [parent(Y,X) = 1] then class = pos
```

This can be transformed into the following DHDB clause as the output of LINUS:

```
daughter(X,Y) :- female(X), parent(Y,X).
```

To demonstrate limitations of the approach, we investigate its application to our running example.

Example 9 *Here, we assume that only two types* numeric *and* nominal *are defined for the running example database. Table* T *is here referred to by the predicate symbol* t. *It has three numeric arguments in the first argument positions and one nominal argument in the last argument position.*

C would then contain the following constrained clauses:

```
t(W,X,Y,Z) :- a(W,W,W,W,Z).
t(W,X,Y,Z) :- a(W,W,W,X,Z).
t(W,X,Y,Z) :- a(W,W,W,Y,Z).
t(W,X,Y,Z) :- a(W,W,X,W,Z).
t(W,X,Y,Z) :- a(W,W,X,X,Z).
```

```
...
t(W,X,Y,Z) :- a(Y,Y,Y,Y,Z).
...
t(W,X,Y,Z) :- b(W,W,W,Z).
...
```

In the first clause, the variable W *for the first numeric argument of* t *is used to fill all argument places for* a, *where numeric values are needed. For the nominal arguments — the last in both relations — the same variable must be shared, here* Z. *In the following clauses, other combinations of shared variables are used.*

These clauses are semantically questionable because there are unifications of unrelated arguments, e. g. for the first clause, the fourth argument of relation a *is a descriptive attribute of objects of kind* a, *which has nothing to do with the identifier attribute of relation* t *in* t *'s first argument position, but the literals for* t *and* a *share a variable in the corresponding argument positions.*

Of course, we could define types differently, e. g. based on the names of attributes. In this case, C *would be empty since each non-target relation encompasses at least one attribute not contained in the target relation. Thus, no variable could be shared here between head and body of a clause. Overall, the application of* LINUS *seems not appropriate here.*

We will return to the case of determinate clauses in C *in the context of* DINUS.

To finish this section, we investigate complexity issues of LINUS. This complexity originates strongly from the usage of variable permutations in the constrained clauses of $\mathcal{C}$. According to Section 5.5 of the ILP book [76] relevant aspects are the following. Given

- u as the number of distinct types of arguments of the target predicate p

- u_i as the number of distinct types of arguments of a background predicate q_i

- $n_{i,s}$ as the number of arguments of q_i of a type T_s

- k_{ArgT_s} as the number of arguments of p of type T_s

Then, the number of new attributes derived from q_i is computed by the following formula:

$$k_{New,q_i} = \prod_{s=1}^{u_i} (k_{ArgT_s})^{n_{i,s}} \tag{3.11}$$

This means that the $n_{i,s}$ places for arguments of q_i of type T_s can be filled in $(k_{ArgT_s})^{n_{i,s}}$ ways independently from choosing the arguments of q_i which are of different types.

We point to the circumstance that results are the same for the usage of determinate literals in $\mathcal{C}$, considering old variables only. New variables have no significant influence on the complexity of $\mathcal{C}$ generation. The same names of new variables can be used in clauses that differ in their usage of old variables only.

If the built-in background predicate for equality =/2 is used, its symmetry is important and thus the number of possible applications amounts to:

$$k_{New,=} = \sum_{s=1}^{u} \binom{k_{ArgT_s}}{2} = \sum_{s=1}^{u} \frac{k_{ArgT_s} \cdot (k_{ArgT_s} - 1)}{2} \tag{3.12}$$

Sums over such terms for all background knowledge predicates, i.e. for all clauses $C \in \mathcal{C}$ lead to the final number of newly derived attributes, which is exponential in the number of body literal arguments of the same type. This demonstrates aspects of the complexity of the generation of clauses for $\mathcal{C}$.

The application of clauses $C \in \mathcal{C}$ is less complex. Before a constrained clause is applied for a certain example e, all variables in the clause are instantiated. The body literal L of C thus becomes ground. It remains to be checked if B contains L. For a clause C known to be determinate, the first matching fact in B for the body literal of C can be found with the same complexity, which is polynomial in the number of old variables in L.

3.2.2 DINUS

Ideas for the DINUS approach were first published in 1992 . The presentation of DINUS provided here is adopted from Section 5.7 of the ILP book by Lavrač and Džeroski [76].

The hypothesis language bias of constrained clauses for LINUS can be weakened to i-determinate clauses, cf. Section 2.3, as implemented in the system DINUS.

DINUS accepts the same input as LINUS, i.e. examples in the form of DHDB clauses and background knowledge in the from of DDB clauses. Let us first consider the case of generating function-free hypotheses. These presuppose Boolean tables as results from propositionalization.

Clauses $C \in \mathcal{C}$ take a special form for DINUS, viz.

$$p(X_1, \ldots, X_n) \; : - \; q_1(X_a, \ldots, X_b, Y_c, \ldots, Y_d),$$
$$\ldots,$$
$$q_m(X_e, \ldots, X_f, Y_g, \ldots, Y_h),$$
$$q_o(X_i, \ldots, X_j).$$

where p is the target predicate and q_x are background knowledge predicates. Literals q_1 to q_m are determinate literals that deliver the values of new variables Y_l

based on bindings of old variables X_k. Literal q_o does not introduce new variables but just consumes old variables.

Note that $m = 0$ is not excluded, though unusual: it would produce a constrained clause $C \in \mathcal{C}$ as used for LINUS. Further, q_o can be left out, though not in the function-free case. We return to this issue below in this section.

As for LINUS, if a call of a clause in $\mathcal{C}$ succeeds for an example, the corresponding feature value is set to *true*, else to *false*. This can be seen as an existential feature in the sense of the framework presented above. Again, $val(C, e, B)$ contains at most one element, because of determinacy. Then, $\varphi_\exists$ is applied as presented in our framework.

The other steps of the DINUS process correspond to those of the LINUS algorithm. The DINUS output takes the form of non-recursive determinate DDB clauses with $p(X_1, X_2, ..., X_n)$ in the head. Converting propositional rules back into first-order rules is based on $\mathcal{C}$ again. Also, post-processing steps such as irrelevant literal elimination are analogous to those for LINUS.

The following example is adopted from sections 5.6.2 and 5.7.1 in [76].

Example 10 *The target relation is* grandmother(X,Y) *and means that person* X *is the grandmother of person* Y. *The task is to define the target relation with the help of the background knowledge relations* father *and* mother. *All variables are of type* person. *To keep the example simple, i-determinacy is used here with* $i = 1$. *Figure 3.3 shows the input data.*

Training examples	Background knowledge		
grandmother(ann,bob). pos	father(zak,tom).	father(pat,ann).	father(zak,jim).
grandmother(ann,sue). pos	mother(ann,tom).	mother(liz,ann).	mother(ann,jim).
grandmother(bob,sue). neg	father(tom,sue).	father(tom,bob).	father(jim,dave).
grandmother(tom,bob). neg	mother(eve,sue).	mother(eve,bob).	mother(jean,dave).

Figure 3.3: A *grandmother* family relationship problem in Prolog form

The literal father(X, A), *where* X *is an old variable, i. e. already bound, while* A *is a new variable, i. e. to be bound, is not determinate: a person can be father of more than one child. However,* father(A, X) *is determinate, since each person has exactly one father. This way, there are the following determinate literals* f(U, X), f(V, Y), m(W, X), m(Z, Y) *that can be used as a first body literal of a clause* $C \in \mathcal{C}$, *where* f *stands for* father *and* m *for* mother.

Those determinate literals contain the variables X, Y, U, V, W, Z *that can be used in the last literal of a clause* $C \in \mathcal{C}$. *Thus, last literals for bodies are the following:* f(U, U), f(U, V), f(U, W), ... *Here, from the Cartesian product of the set of variables with itself, only those combinations of variables are missing that occur as argument pairs in the four determinate literals listed above. An element from the set of possible last literals can be introduced, subject to the restriction to contain old variables only.*

Thus, $\mathcal{C}$ *contains clauses:*

1. *grandmother(X,Y) :- father(U,X), mother(U,U).*

2. *grandmother(X,Y) :- father(U,X), mother(U,X).*

3. *grandmother(X,Y) :- father(U,X), mother(U,Y).*

4. *grandmother(X,Y) :- father(V,Y), mother(V,V).*

5. *...*

Figure 3.4 shows the results of first determining the values of the variables with the help of the determinate literals in the clauses in C and then the truth values for the final literals of those clauses.

Variables		New variables					Propositional features			
X	Y	f(U,X)	f(V,Y)	m(W,X)	m(Z,Y)	...	m(X,V)	m(X,Z)	...	class
ann	bob	pat	tom	liz	eve		1	0		pos
ann	sue	pat	tom	liz	eve		1	0		pos
bob	sue	tom	tom	eve	eve		0	0		neg
tom	bob	zak	tom	ann	eve		0	0		neg

Figure 3.4. Propositional form of the *grandmother* relationship problem (1 for *true*, 0 for *false*; new variables are listed within the literals that introduce them)

From the propositional representation, an attribute value learner may induce a rule such as the following:

```
if [mother(X,V) = 1] then class = pos
```

This rule is transcribed into the clause:

```
grandmother(X,Y) :- mother(X,V).
```

The new variable V must be introduced by a determinate literal, viz. father(V,Y). The result is hence:

```
grandmother(X,Y) :- father(V, Y), mother(X,V).
```

Obviously, this is not a complete definition of the usual grandmother relation since the mother's mother relationship is not included. Since the parts of the example provided above already illustrate the workings of DINUS *sufficiently, we do not go into more details here.*

We demonstrate limitations of DINUS with the help of our running example.

Example 11 *Let us assume that the tables of the running example are completely specified, i. e. "..." should not be present. Let us further assume two types numeric and nominal, defined in a way usual for machine learning.*

For the construction of $\mathcal{C}$, DINUS *would first determine all determinate literals. The following clauses would be investigated:*

```
t(W,X,Y,Z)  :- a(W,A,B,C,D).
t(W,X,Y,Z)  :- a(A,W,B,C,D).
...
```

Remember that the first argument is always an identifier for the elements of the corresponding relation. While a(W, A, B, C) *is determinate, the correspondence of the identifiers of relation* t *and relation* a *is semantically questionable.*

On the other hand, a(A, W, B, C) *is semantically justified by the corresponding foreign key relationship, but it is not determinate, mirroring the one-to-many-relationship between* t *and* a.

The only literals which are both semantically justifiable and determinate are f(X, A, B, C, D) *and* g(Y, A, B) *because of the many-to-one-relationships between* t *and* f *and between* t *and* g.

As a second step, for each clause, a last literal has to be built that consumes the variables newly introduced by the other literals constructed before. Here, it is not possible to find any that are semantically justifiable, for the same reasons as shown above in the process to find determinate literals. Thus, $\mathcal{C}$ *better remains empty.*

If we define types differently, e. g. based on the names of attributes, $\mathcal{C}$ *would again be empty: the last literals of each clause would have to be the same as one of the literals occurring before in the clause, in order to make type strictness possible. However, this does not lead to desired results. Overall, the application of* DINUS *restricted to function-free clauses as presented above seems not appropriate here.*

According to the literature, it seems unusual to drop the restriction to function-free hypotheses. We drop it for our experimental work. Thus, results of propositionalization may include non-Boolean features. Here, a clause $C \in \mathcal{C}$ takes the form

$$p(X_1, \ldots, X_n) \quad :- \quad q_1(X_a, \ldots, X_b, Y_c, \ldots, Y_d),$$
$$\ldots,$$
$$q_m(X_e, \ldots, X_f, Y_g, \ldots, Y_h).$$

with the same meaning as for the function-free case. Especially, X_k stand for old variables and Y_l for new variables. Note the missing last literal from the function-free case, q_o.

If a call of a clause $C \in \mathcal{C}$ succeeds for an example, the corresponding feature value(s) is / are set to the values of the new variable(s) of the body literal. More elaborate, $val(C, e, B)$ contains at most one element, because of determinacy. The propositionalization function used here is identity φ_{id}, i.e. values of new variables in determinate literals are directly used as new attribute values.

Thus, this variant corresponds largely to using LINUS with determinate clauses in $\mathcal{C}$. However, LINUS is restricted to using only one body literal in each clause $C \in \mathcal{C}$. If this restriction would be alleviated, there would still be the restriction to 1-determinate clauses in $\mathcal{C}$ for LINUS.

Example 12 *We continue Example 11. If we remove the function-free restriction, we have both the values from* t *tuples and the values for* A, B, C, D *from the application of* t(X,Y,Z) :- f(X, A, B, C, D), *among others, contained in the table that results from propositionalization.*

The complexity of DINUS originates again strongly from the kind of usage of variables in the clauses of $\mathcal{C}$. In the general case, $\mathcal{C}$ for DINUS is a superset of that for LINUS, such that it is obvious that there is again an exponential behavior of the number of clauses.

3.2.3   Propositionalization based on PROGOL

In 1996, Srinivasan and King presented an approach for propositionalization that uses PROGOL [88] for propositionalization. Later, an extended description was provided by the same authors [121]. The authors try to enhance expert provided features for learning problems in the domain of biochemistry with Boolean features constructed from PROGOL clauses, which are first learned from examples and background knowledge. Among the learning tasks are some derived from the Mutagenicity problem [123], cf. Appendix B.

The approach was the first to accommodate arbitrary background knowledge, i.e. especially the non-determinate case, and it easily extends to other ILP learning systems and to other domains. Initially, PROGOL with its usual potential of inputs, cf. Section 2.3, is used to arrive at clauses that describe properties of examples in terms of background knowledge. This process is carried out for each class of examples, with those examples of the focused class as positive examples and the examples of other classes as negative examples. The clauses do not have to explain all the examples.

From the clauses learned by PROGOL, all of which have $\top$ as head, clauses $C \in \mathcal{C}$ are derived by using subsets of the body literals, subject to the constraint that resulting clauses are linked, cf. Definition 8. From those clauses, a subset is selected based on the criterion of compression of the corresponding ILP clauses. Results of calls of these clauses are again treated with $\varphi_\exists$ as shown in our framework.

Srinivasan and King provide the following example [121, Fig. 2], here adopted to our framework.

Example 13 *Let us assume,* PROGOL *produced the following clause from examples and background knowledge:*

```
active(A) :- has_rings(A,[R1,R2,R3]), hydrophob(A,H), H > 2.1.
```

Then, the following clauses are produced as a basis for C.

```
active(A) :- has_rings(A,[R1,R2,R3]).
active(A) :- hydrophob(A,H).
active(A) :- has_rings(A,[R1,R2,R3]), hydrophob(A,H).
active(A) :- hydrophob(A,H), H > 2.1.
active(A) :- has_rings(A,[R1,R2,R3]), hydrophob(A,H), H > 2.1.
```

Trivial clauses such as the second, which will usually hold for all molecules, are discarded by the clause selection procedure mentioned above. The other clauses are used to compute the corresponding feature values for the examples.

All produced features are Boolean here. Originally, they were used to enhance input tables for regression, but they are not limited to that purpose. For regression, the features turned out to be useful enhancements in some cases.

Complexity of $\mathcal{C}$ generation originates mainly from two sources: first, the application of PROGOL, to arrive at a set of clauses, which is in a second step further processed into more clauses used as feature definitions. The user can restrict especially the size of the latter set of clauses, although finding appropriate settings might be non-trivial in practice.

Complexity of $\mathcal{C}$ application can grow exponentially with the number of background predicates. More on join complexity will follow in Chapter 5. In practice, the number of body literals in clauses is restricted by another parameter, which must be set by the user.

3.2.4   Propositionalization based on WARMR

The approach WARMR for mining association rules in multiple relations was first presented by Dehaspe and De Raedt in 1997 [27]. More detailed presentations followed [28].

Different from PROGOL, WARMR does not intend to learn predictive models but rather descriptive models. At an early stage of the application of WARMR, the system constructs queries as conjunctions of literals according to mode and type declarations similar to those of PROGOL. Queries that succeed for a sufficient number of examples are further processed, mainly to form so-called query extensions that correspond to association rules in the single relational case.

Another way of further processing is taken when those queries are used to construct Boolean features for the examples. Here, feature values are set to 1 for an example, if the corresponding query succeeds for that example, and to 0 otherwise. The intuition behind the approach lies in the assumption that queries that succeed with a certain frequency would be a good basis for the construction of relevant features.

There are hints at the opportunity of this kind of usage of WARMR results in many papers on that system and also hints at realizations of the approach in the context of the Predictive Evaluation Challenge [122].

From each query as typical for WARMR, a clause $C \in \mathcal{C}$ can be constructed by taking the first literal as head and the remaining literals as body. With such a construction of $\mathcal{C}$, we have again a correspondence to applying $\varphi_\exists$ to results of calls of the elements of this set as presented in our framework above.

An example provided by Dehaspe and Toivonen [28] is the following.

Example 14 *Figure 3.5 shows a Prolog database with customer information. The headings "training examples" and "background knowledge" are introduced here to allow for a better comparison with example data provided above in the context of* LINUS/DINUS. *Note that missing class labels would not allow for learning classifiers here.*

Training examples	Background knowledge	
customer(allen).	parent(allen,bill).	buys(allen,wine).
customer(bill).	parent(allen,carol).	buys(bill,cola).
customer(carol).	parent(bill,zoe).	buys(bill,pizza).
customer(diana).	parent(carol,diana).	buys(diana,pizza).

Figure 3.5: Prolog database with customer information

From queries that could be produced using appropriate mode and type declarations, we can arrive at the following $\mathcal{C}$.

```
customer(X)  :- parent(X,Y), buys(Y,cola).
customer(X)  :- parent(X,Y).
customer(X)  :- parent(X,Y), buys(Y,wine).
customer(X)  :- buys(X,Y).
```

Then, the application of our function prop *— adopted to the case without class information — would result in the table as depicted in Fig. 3.6.*

Based on results such as the table in the example, learning tasks such as clustering can be tackled.

The complexity of this method for propositionalization is due to both WARMR datalog query construction and computing their answers. Especially the latter might be costly, depending on the number and kind of relations involved. More information and examples for join complexities follow in Chapter 5.

Id	Q1Attr	Q2Attr	Q3Attr	Q4Attr
allen	1	1	0	1
bill	0	1	0	1
carol	0	1	0	0
diana	0	0	0	1

Figure 3.6: A table resulting from propositionalization with WARMR for the customer database

3.2.5   Stochastic Propositionalization

Stochastic Propositionalization (SP) was first presented in 1998 [61]. The presentation provided here is based on both that paper and the PhD dissertation by Kramer [58]. SP was the first general-purpose algorithm to deal with nondeterminate background knowledge, without using other ILP systems like PROGOL or WARMR.

The algorithm for SP accepts the same kind of inputs as the systems for propositionalization shown above, and then starts refining the most general clause $\top : -true$. This is done similar to genetic algorithms. For a good introduction to genetic algorithms, the reader is referred to the presentation by Mitchell [84].

For a number of steps of SP, a certain percentage of the clauses is removed probabilistically based on a fitness function and replaced by random refinements of parent clauses, which are also chosen based on quality considerations.

The refinement operator within SP is defined in terms of schemata, which declare that certain literals may be added to certain clauses considering variable bindings and types. For classification, an evaluation of clauses is based on the Minimum Description Length (MDL) principle as described by Rissanen [110].

The quality of the new generation of clauses is compared to that of the generation before, to either replace it or not. The fitness of a set of clauses is defined in a special way.

Note that the clauses handled by SP can be regarded as a set $\mathcal{C}$. Finally, they are used with $\varphi_\exists$ to arrive at Boolean features.

Since there can be a large number of features for a given learning problem, a selection is proposed to be made based on the following constraints that the constructed clauses for features should be

C1 not too specific or too general

C2 not too complex

C3 different from one another

C4 different from existing, expert-provided features

The reasons for C3 and C4 seem obvious, viz. the avoidance of redundancy. However, it is not clear *a priori*, if C1 and C2 are appropriate constraints in all

learning situations. They can be regarded as intuitive heuristics that turned out
to be useful in a number of applications.

Those criteria are intended to be fulfilled here by the following measures

C1 parameters control the required minimum and maximum coverage of clauses

C2 the MDL principle is used to evaluate clauses; furthermore, parameters
restrict the maximum number of variables, and no negation is used in the
clauses

C3 the algorithm considers only refinements that yield clauses the extension of
which has to differ in at least one example from the extensions of clauses
in the current population

C4 same measure as for C3

SP was applied, among others, in the Mutagenicity domain [123], for which
the following example was provided.

Example 15 *The application of SP resulted in features [58] such as*

```
active(A) :- atm(A, B, _, 27, _),
             sym_bond(A, B, C, _),
             atm(A, C, _, 29, _).
```

*The corresponding feature is "true" if in compound A there exists a bond
between an atom of type 27 and an atom of type 29.*

*Note the usage of anonymous variables "_" here, instead of neglecting values
of new variables, as could be done in other approaches to propositionalization
such as those presented above.*

Kramer further points out that a clause $C \in \mathcal{C}$ should have the ability to
partition the data here, while in usual ILP learning e.g. with FOIL, coverage is
the measurement of interest. Further, he shows that SP can be updated to be a
non-propositional ILP learner.

However, in the base version, Kramer [58] mainly applies C4.5rules [104] as
a propositional learner on the result of SP because it outperformed C4.5 as used
before [61]. The learning results are not transformed back into Prolog rules.

The complexity of the algorithm is high as revealed in empirical work. This
could be expected for an approach drawing strongly from ideas in the field of
genetic algorithms.

A positive effect of stochastic refinements can be seen in the potentially deep
features, i.e. those based on clauses from $\mathcal{C}$ with many body literals. They would
usually not be produced within other approaches. There, a language bias must
often be chosen that does not allow for clauses with many literals, in order to
achieve any results within an acceptable time at all.

3.2.6   Extended Transformation Approach

An extension of LINUS to allow for learning non-determinate DHDB clauses was
first presented by Flach and Lavrač in 2000 and further elaborated by the same
authors in 2001 [77]. We adopt that presentation here within our framework and
concentrate on the central propositionalization steps.

As input, extended LINUS accepts the same kind of descriptions of examples
and background knowledge as the original version of LINUS. Those descriptions
can take the form of structured Prolog clauses, usually ground for examples,
possibly non-ground and even recursive for background knowledge.

Usually, the background knowledge predicates take the form of two-place predicates. This cirumstance means no win or loss in expressiveness as we will demonstrate later in this section.

Clauses $C \in \mathcal{C}$ then take the following form:

$$
\top \quad :- \quad s_i(X, Y),
$$
$$
\ldots,
$$
$$
u_j(X, a),
$$
$$
\ldots
$$

Each clause must be linked, cf. Definition 8. It has $\top$ as head, as formulated
in our framework. Further, the body of each clause $C \in \mathcal{C}$ contains zero or
more function-free literals, i. e. with two variables as arguments, and one or more
literals with one variable and one constant as arguments.

Literals can also occur in their negated form, which adds to the expressiveness
of the features produced, as emphasized by Lavrač and Flach [77].

Typically, certain syntactic restrictions are put on the clauses $C \in \mathcal{C}$, e. g. a
maximum number of literals and/or a maximum number of variables. Within
this bias, the generation of $\mathcal{C}$ is usually exhaustive.

As for LINUS, if a call of a clause in $\mathcal{C}$ succeeds for an example, the corresponding feature value is set to *true*, else to *false*. This can be seen as an existential
feature in the sense of the framework presented above. Here, $val(C, e, B)$ will
often be a set of size greater than one because of the allowed non-determinacy.
However, because of the restrictions imposed by the literals containing const-
nants, the set will often be small. In any case, $\varphi_\exists$ can be applied here exactly as
presented in our framework.

The following example is provided in section 4.2 of the article by Lavrač and
Flach [77]. It is based on the East-West Challenge [81, 83]. The learning task is to
discover models of low complexity that classify trains as eastbound or westbound.
The problem is illustrated in Figure B.1, cf. Appendix B. The reader can find a
non-flattened representation there, as well.

Example 16 *With a flattened representation using non-structured ground facts,
the first train in Figure B.1 can be represented as follows:*

```
east(t1).
```

```
hasCar(t1,c11).          hasCar(t1,c12).
cshape(c11,rect).        cshape(c12,rect).
clength(c11,short).      clength(c12,long).
cwall(c11,single).       cwall(c12,single).
croof(c11,none).         croof(c12,none).
cwheels(c11,2).          cwheels(c12,3).
hasLoad(c11,l11).        hasLoad(c12,l12).
lshape(l11,circ).        lshape(l12,hexa).
lnumber(l11,1).          lnumber(l12,1).


hasCar(t1,c13).          hasCar(t1,c14).
cshape(c13,rect).        cshape(c14,rect).
clength(c13,short).      clength(c14,long).
cwall(c13,single).       cwall(c14,single).
croof(c13,peak).         croof(c14,none).
cwheels(c13,2).          cwheels(c14,2).
hasLoad(c13,l13).        hasLoad(c14,l14).
lshapo(l13,tria).        lshape(l14,rect).
lnumber(l13,1).          lnumber(l14,3).
```

Non-flattened and flattened representations are not equivalent here, since order information is missing in the latter. This is one of the occasions of information loss during preparation of the data for propositionalization as pointed to in the description of our framework.

Literals can be introduced into a clause $C \in \mathcal{C}$ according to type restrictions and up to certain numbers of literals and variables. For instance, in such a bias allowing for 3 literals and 2 variables and with the flattened representation, clauses for $\mathcal{C}$ as the following can be constructed.

```
east(T) :- hasCar(T,C), clength(C,short).
east(T) :- hasCar(T,C), not croof(C,none).
```

For the trains example, there are 190 such clauses with up to two literals with constants, and with up to two body variables that not occur in the head.

Lavrač and Flach [77] report, that they applied CN2 on the Boolean table resulting from the calls of $C \in \mathcal{C}$ and finally arrived at the following rule, among others, where each body line mirrors a clause $C \in \mathcal{C}$:

```
east(T):-
   hasCar(T,C1),hasLoad(C1,L1),lshape(L1,tria),lnumber(L1,1),
   not (hasCar(T,C2),clength(C2,long),croof(C2,jagged)),
   not (hasCar(T,C3),hasLoad(C3,L3),clength(C3,long),lshape(L3,circ)).
```

If negation is allowed within features, the following simple rule is induced:

```
east(T):-
   hasCar(T,C),clength(C,short),not croof(C,none).
```

This means that a train is eastbound if and only if it has a short closed car. Note the usage of the 10-trains-problem here, in contrast to the 20-trains-problem as dealt with below in our experimental sections.

In the following, we continue the example, investigating another representation of the examples and background knowledge, which is accommodated by our framework.

Example 17 *For the trains problem, a typical representation in a relational database would use two or three relations:* train, car, *and possibly* load, *cf. Appendix B. (The relation for trains contains class information in an extra attribute, here.) Thus, in* C *there would be the following clauses instead of those given above, making use of anonymous variables.*

```
train(T,Bound) :- car(_,T,_,short,_,_,_).
train(T,Bound) :- not car(_,T,_,_,_,none,_).
```

A transformation from the relational database representation to two place predicates is simple, consider the following example.

```
hasCar(T,C)  :- train(T,_), car(T,C,_,_,_,_,_).
clenght(C,L) :- car(_,C,_,L,_,_,_).
```

A transformation such as this is discussed by Morik and Brockhausen [85], there as "mapping 2" of several possible mappings from a relational database to logical representations. However, this transformation adds to the complexity of the procedure and maybe forces the user to make the appropriate declarations.

Declarations could be produced automatically though, making use of attribute name information from the relational database schema, among others, as actually done for our experiments below, cf. Appendix A.

A non-flattened, term-based representation can also be constructed from a relational database, when row numbers indicate orders e. g. of cars in trains.

We now demonstrate the special power of extended LINUS with the help of our running example.

Example 18 *With the appropriate declarations of types, background knowledge predicates, and parameter settings for maximum number of literals and variables in the clauses $C \in C$, extended* LINUS *can build a number of clauses for* C *from the running example database, e. g. the following, very much like it treated the trains problem above, here in the notation favored for the framework.*

```
t(T,_,_,Class) :- a(A,T,_,_,y), b(_,A,300,_).
```

This feature definition would — with respect to each example — ask for a related substructure in relation a *to have value* y *for attribute* A_cat *and to have a further substructure described in relation* b *which in turn shows value 300 for attribute* B_num.

Meanwhile, there are several implementations of the extended LINUS approach available, e.g. the system RSD [78], and also the system SINUS [67]. These systems implement advanced strategies to deal with the complexity of the approach. For instance, RSD implements a search for clauses in $\mathcal{C}$ that uses class information. This allows for the application of pruning strategies. It can be seen as a form of supervised propositionalization.

In general, apart from the possibly critical number of clauses in $\mathcal{C}$, processing of those clauses, i.e. their calls, can become expensive, cf. considerations of joins in Chapter 5.

3.2.7 Further Approaches

RL-ICET

For the East-West Challenge in 1994 [83], cf. Appendix B, Turney developed a solution that can be seen as a first instance of propositionalization for non-determinate background knowledge [126], although in a task-specific way. For his system RL-ICET (Relational Learning with ICET, a hybrid of a genetic algorithm and a decision tree induction algorithm), Turney preprocesses the trains data with a strong influence of the challenge task documentation. For instance, he defines clauses equivalent to a clause $C \in \mathcal{C}$ as in our framework:

```
trains(T,Bound) :- has_car(T,C), ellipse(C).
```

to test for the circumstance that an arbitrary car of a train has elliptical shape. Again, the application of this clause conforms to our $\varphi_\exists$. Turney reports that he defined at first 28 such clauses or features, respectively, obviously for the different values the attributes such as *shape* can take. Then, he combined bodies of those clauses conjunctively, e.g. for *ellipse_triangle_load* to test for a car with elliptical shape and a load of triangle shape, into 378 more clauses.

In addition, Turney introduced a special predicate *infront(T,C1,C2)* to form even more features such as *u_shaped_infront_peaked_roof*, resulting in 784 more clauses. Finally, he added 9 clauses for general features of trains such as *trains_4* to become true iff a train has exactly 4 cars. Overall, 1,199 clauses were used.

The binary features are then input for propositional learning, more precisely decision tree learning. Learning takes the complexity of the clauses in $\mathcal{C}$ into account as well, in terms of the number of their literals and terms. This is done to achieve the final aim of a less complex theory, which in turn is achieved by building Prolog rules manually from the decision trees that were learned.

In conclusion on RL-ICET, extended LINUS as presented above can be seen as a generalization of Turney's special purpose approach.

Bottom-up Propositionalization

Bottom-up propositionalization was presented by Kramer and Frank in 2000 [59]. It is tailored for biochemical databases. More specifically, the objective is the discovery of frequent 2D fragments in molecules. Search proceeds in a domain-specific way.

The approach is related to both PROGOL and WARMR. First, because the generation of fragment features is controlled bottom-up, i. e. example-/data-driven, as in PROGOL, to generate only fragments that really exist in the data. Second, the aim to discover frequent items is also an objective for WARMR, resulting in specific approaches.

The generated fragments can be regarded as clauses $C \in \mathcal{C}$ that are handled with φ_3 from our framework. It is also interesting to note that support-vector machines are applied here, because they are supposed to be able to deal with a large number of moderately relevant features. A conversion of the learning results back to Prolog form is not intended here.

In 2001, Kramer and De Raedt presented more work on feature construction in biochemical domains [62]. Here, the user can specify constraints such as on the frequency of features, also separately for positive and negative examples, and on the generality of features. The solution space for such constraints is a version space, cf. Mitchell [84], which makes it possible to apply corresponding algorithms.

Empirical work shows that models can be found efficiently here, which are competitive with results of other approaches, e. g. with accuracies of more than 93% on the Mutagenesis data set with 188 examples, cf. Appendix B and our empirical results for this learning task. However, the restriction to the biochemical domain seems strong for the approach.

Lazy Propositionalization

Alphonse and Rouveirol introduced another kind of propositionalization called lazy propositionalization [4]. It is different from the approaches presented so far in several aspects. First, there is usually more than one tuple constructed from the relational representation of an example. This excludes the application of conventional data mining systems. Thus, it is not propositionalization in our sense, cf. Definition 9. Second, not all examples are processed, but decisions are taken during AQ-like learning, which Boolean examples should be produced to effectively and efficiently discriminate classes.

The authors point out that FOL learning problems can be decomposed into two sub-problems, viz. a relational or structural one and a functional one. While the first leads to the construction of Boolean features, the second leads to also otherwise valued features. However, the focus of their research is then put on the relational part such that we have again an instance of the framework using $\varphi_\exists$, where clauses $C \in \mathcal{C}$ are constructed from structured examples.

The system PROPAL implements the ideas of lazy propositionalization. A result on the Mutagenesis problem (188 instances) is reported, viz. an accuracy of 83%, which is competitive compared to the general purpose ILP systems FOIL, PROGOL, and TILDE.

Latest Developments

An approach to propositionalization for clustering is introduced by Bournaud and colleagues [17]. The authors deal with a graphical formalism and search example graphs for subgraphs of decreasing abstraction levels. Subgraph descriptions can be reformulated as clauses, such that we have again a case of a certain construction of a set $\mathcal{C}$ as a basis for propositionalization and $\varphi_\exists$ as a main part of the propositionalization function. Experiments were carried out to cluster Chinese characters.

Following ideas of WARMR, Blaťák and Popelínsky [12] propose a partial search for maximal queries for propositionalization. They show its applicability and results for the Mutagenicity problem, among others. The authors focus on the learning problem with 188 examples, cf. Appendix B and elsewhere in this thesis. They achieve accuracies of up to almost 88%. However, the algorithm seems complex considering the long execution times provided here with $> 10,000$ sec.

Pfahringer and Holmes [98] again work in a graph-oriented formalism and especially on biochemical learning problems with their approach to propositionalization by stochastic discrimination (SD). A construction of subgraphs is guided by examples, similar to the workings of PROGOL. Those subgraphs can again be regarded as a different notation for clauses $C \in \mathcal{C}$, and $\varphi_\exists$ is applied. Remarkably, extensive use of counts of subgraphs is also made for the propositionalization results, i.e. $\varphi_\#$ as given as an example in the presentation of our framework above. For the Mutagenicity problem (188 examples), they report better results for using counts than for using Boolean features only, up to an accuracy of more than 87%. Runtimes are not provided here.

3.3 Summary

As was shown in this chapter, there are a series of different approaches to propositionalization in the context of Inductive Logic Programming. Still, the variants are not exhaustively investigated, consider the following example. In a simi-

Table 3.1: Properties of approaches to propositionalization (grouping for better readability)

Approach	Year	Domain	Complete	Supervised	Hypo.-Language
QUMAS	1989	medical	n. i.	n. i.	not investigated
LINUS	1990	general	possible	no	constrained
DINUS	1992	general	possible	no	determinate
RL-ICET	1995	trains	no	no	domain-specific
PROGOL	1996	general	no	yes	arbitrary
WARMR	1997	general	possible	possible	arbitrary
SP	1998	general	no	yes	arbitrary
EXT. LINUS	2000	general	no	no	arbitrary
BOTTOM-UP	2000	biochem.	no	yes	domain-specific
PROPAL	2000	general	no	yes	arbitrary
RSD	2002	general	no	yes	arbitrary
SD	2003	biochem.	no	no	domain-specific

lar way to the usage of PROGOL and WARMR for propositionalization, other systems such as MIDOS [133] could be used for propositionalization. Here, supervised learning of local models with descriptive character could be an interesting starting point.

Table 3.1 gives an overview of properties of approaches to propositionalization. We see a continuing effort to develop approaches in the field within the last nearly 20 years. Originating from special-purpose approaches, general applicability was achieved for some approaches. Domain-specific systems remain competitive, though. Usually, systems have to abstain from completeness for efficiency reasons.

Depending on the supervised or unsupervised character of propositionalization, care must be taken of the details of learning, e. g. the moment when to partition data for cross-validation. This should happen *before* propositionalization for supervised methods. It can be *after* propositionalization for unsupervised methods. Finally, the approaches can be distinguished with respect to the different expressive power of their inputs and outputs.

We observe for the traditional approaches to propositionalization that they usually have the potential for producing non-Boolean features. However, this is rarely used. Exactly this predominant usage of $\varphi_\exists$ as mentioned in our framework leads us to see all those approaches in the LINUS tradition, hence the qualification as "traditional".

The complexity of the approaches is usually high, often exponential in parameters such as the number of variables of the same type or the number of relations, in at least one of the two phases clause generation or clause application.

With respect to the 3E criteria, the approaches dealt with in this chapter have shown remarkable effectiveness. Efficiency was often not in the focus of the earlier investigations. Observing complexities of the algorithms, efficiency is not satisfactory yet. The same holds for usability, where some systems cannot be applied to relevant real-life databases, especially those with high degrees of non-determinacy in the data, while others demand for partly laborios and ultimately non-trivial specifications of restrictions for languages and search processes.

Considering the criteria for a framework that were formulated at the beginning of this chapter, our framework largely fulfilled the first two criteria. The framework allowed for precise and unified descriptions of the essentials of different approaches to propositionalization. Also, a comparison of the approaches under a series of viewpoints as exemplified by the usage of different kinds of φ for propositionalization was possible.

The third criterion w. r. t. extensibility of existing approaches is the topic of the following chapter.

Chapter 4

Aggregation-based Propositionalization

In this chapter, we present our approach to propositionalization, which builds up on our framework presented in the preceding chapter. The main objective of our approach is to arrive at better 3E properties.

First, we introduce our ideas for sets of clauses $\mathcal{C}$ for propositionalization. Here, we exploit foreign links as introduced for the system MIDOS [133]. We further use functional dependencies between relations or rather their elements [71]. This topic has a strong influence on efficiency of the approach.

Second, we explain our choices of functions φ for propositionalization, which are influenced by the frequent usage of aggregate functions in database systems. Based on these components, we describe our algorithm for propositionalization [71]. This subject is most relevant for effectivity of propositionalization.

Third, two closely related approaches — ROLLUP [54] and Relational Concept Classes [96] — are reviewed and compared to our approach.

Finally, we offer an extensive empirical investigation into properties of our approach and compare to results of both prominent ILP systems and other systems for propositionalization. The discussion includes views at further related work as well.

4.1 Clause Sets for Propositionalization

4.1.1 Generation of Clauses

An important aspect of propositionalization is the set of clauses $\mathcal{C}$ that forms its basis. The range of choices is wide, and decisions here have an impact on the complexity of the whole process, since both clause set generation and its further usage can be expensive. Let us give some examples for clauses in the view of our running example, cf. Appendix D.

Example 19 *Examples for clauses that could be in* $\mathcal{C}$ *are the following, with variable names mostly as abbreviations of the original column names:*

1. *t(T,F,G,Class) :- a(T,T,T,T,Class).*

2. *t(T,F,G,Class) :- g(G,Gn,Gc).*

3. *t(T,F,G,Class) :- a(A,T,C,An,Ac), b(B,A,Bn,Bc).*

4. *t(T,F,G,Class) :- a(A,T,C,An,x), b(B,A,Bn,Bc).*

5. *t(T,F,G,Class) :- a(A1,T,C1,An1,x), a(A2,T,C2,An2,y).*

Clause 1 is an example of a constrained clause as used in LINUS, where variables in the body must occur in the head of the clause. The foreign key relationship in the original database is correctly modeled here by variable T *occuring in the second argument position of literal* a. *However, also sharing this variable in other argument positions causes the semantics of this clause to be rather questionable. Similarly, sharing Class between the* t *and* a *literals seems not appropriate.*

Clause 2 is an example of a determinate clause as typically used in DINUS, where local variables in the body must have a unique binding given a binding of the global variables in the head. This is the case here because of the many-to-one relationship between tables t *and* g.

The other three example clauses 3 to 5 also share variables corresponding to foreign key relationships. Sharing variables in this way corresponds to a basis for computing natural joins. The first clause has variables in all argument places while the second and third example clauses also contain constants in argument places which correspond to selection criteria. Note that example clause 5 makes multiple use of literals derived from relation a.

The intuition behind our approach to clause set generation for propositionalization is the following. If possible, all relations should be included in at least one of the clauses, since their contribution to final models is not known *a priori*. Further, inclusion should be kept simple in order to allow for efficiency.

In order to decide which clause set $\mathcal{C}$ to use as the basis of our transformation, consider again the nature of many relational databases such as business databases. Typically, they will exploit foreign key relationships to structure their data. We have therefore chosen to generate the set $\mathcal{C}$ on the basis of the *foreign link* bias language which was first introduced in MIDOS [133, 135] and allows to easily model the structure of such databases.

This bias is an ordered set of links $\mathcal{L}$, where each $l \in \mathcal{L}$ provides information about the argument positions of literals of two predicates where variables may be shared.

As an additional level of control, our declarative bias language allows the specification of an upper limit on the number of literals with which a given literal

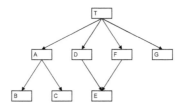

Figure 4.1: The running example database schema overview (arrows represent foreign links)

may share variables. This limit effectively controls the *branching factor* in the graph of literals generated by the foreign links. We again illustrate with the help of our running example.

Example 20 *Figure 4.1 depicts the tables from database in Figure D.1, without columns for better readability. Here, arrows represent foreign links. They form paths in the graph from the target relation to the other relations and can be defined by the user based on a subset of the foreign key relationships in the database. Note that the graph is an acyclic directed graph.*

A number of further restrictions is implemented in our algorithm for propositionalization, which is shown in Section 4.3.

The usage of acyclic graphs presents one of the restrictions that we apply. The user, who has to provide foreign link specifications, must take decisions how to deal with circles in the undirected graph induced by the relational database. We will come back to this issue in Chapter 5.

Another restriction we use in order to keep a clause set $\mathcal{C}$ small is that we do not allow for several literals with the same predicate name in a clause $C \in \mathcal{C}$. Also, a literal derived from the target relation is not allowed in clause bodies.

Note that in principle, foreign links are not restricted to model aspects of foreign key relationships but arbitrary joins of relations or predicates.

Further, we point to the close relationship of foreign links with function-free, two-place body literals in clauses $C \in \mathcal{C}$ for extended LINUS, and similar constructs for several other ILP systems such as special mode declarations for PRO-GOL. Foreign links seem more directly related to work with relational databases, though.

4.1.2   Elimination of Clauses

An important class of propositionalization functions is the class of *local* propositionalization functions which compute propositional features taking into account only one of the variables at a time.

φ is *local* iff there is a function φ' such that

$$\varphi(C, val(C, e, B)) = \bigoplus_{i=1..|vars(C)|} \varphi'(\pi_i(val(C, e, B))) \ , \qquad (4.1)$$

where π_i denotes projection on the i-th column.

This class of propositionalization functions is important because it easily allows the removal of redundant features whenever there are *functional dependencies* between a single predicate (or set of predicates) and another predicate.

If D is a set of atoms, L an atom, then $D \triangleright L$ is a *functional dependency* iff for any σ such that

$$D\sigma \subseteq E \cup B \ , \qquad (4.2)$$

there is *exactly* one θ such that

$$L\sigma\theta \in E \cup B \ . \qquad (4.3)$$

Note that functional dependencies are closely related to the idea of *determinate literals* [89], except that for determinate literals, one often allows *at most* one substitution given the preceding literals, whereas a functional dependency requires that there be *exactly* one such substitution.[1]

For local propositionalization functions, we can drop all the features generated based on one clause if there is another clause which differs from it only in that it contains an additional functionally dependent literal. The reason for this is expressed in the following lemma.

Lemma Let C and C' be two clauses from $\mathcal{C}$ such that

$$C' = C \cup \{L\} \ . \qquad (4.4)$$

If there is a functional dependency $D \triangleright L$ with

$$D\sigma \subseteq C \qquad (4.5)$$

(D subsumes C), then for any *local* φ, and any p-atom e,

$$\varphi(C', val(C', e, B)) = \varphi(C, val(C, e, B)) \bigoplus_{z \in V_L} \varphi'(\pi_z(val(C', e, B))) \ , \quad (4.6)$$

where we assume that V_L are the indexes of variables in $vars(C')$, restricted to variables that do not occur in C.

---

[1] For RDB, functional dependency denotes relationships of (sets of) attributes within one relation, which is different from our notion. Further, it may be useful to think of our concept of functional dependency as *strong determinacy*, while determinacy as defined in Section 2.3 could be called *weak determinacy*.

Proof Clearly, due to the functional dependency, for any variable binding tuple in $val(C, e, B)$ there will be exactly one completion resulting in a matching tuple in $val(C', e, B)$. This means that $val(C, e, B)$ and $val(C', e, B)$ are different, but since the transformation function is local, the extra columns in $val(C', e, B)$ do not influence the computation of the feature values on variables contained in both C and C', so the feature values computed for these variables with respect to C and C' will be identical.

This means, it suffices to consider C' when constructing $prop(\mathcal{C}, e, B)$ since the features constructed based on C will be redundant.

In our approach, we assume that the functional dependencies are explicitly given by the user. However, it will of course also be possible to use one of the existing algorithms for functional dependency discovery [7, 46] to automate this step.

In order to exploit the potential offered by the Lemma above for avoiding the production of redundant features, we thus allow the user to specify a set of functional dependencies $\mathcal{F}$. To achieve that, the user can exploit his or her knowledge about many-to-one relationships between tables in the database along foreign links.

An illustrative example will follow in Section 4.3.

4.2   Query Result Processing

A challenge in propositionalizing relational data is due to the non-determinacy of most applications. In the terminology introduced in the preceding chapter, this means that $val(C, e, B)$ can become quite a large set. This is especially true in business applications, where it is quite possible, for example, that a company maintains hundreds of transactions on record for a single customer. Previous approaches to propositionalization in ILP that were restricted to determinate clauses thus cannot adequately handle such datasets.

In order to design our approach to transformation-based ILP learning, we have therefore borrowed the idea of *aggregation* that is commonplace in the database area [21] and often used in preprocessing for propositional learners. Aggregation is an operation that replaces a (multi-)set of values by a suitable single value that summarizes properties of the set. For numeric values, simple statistical descriptors such as average, maximum, and minimum can be used, for nominal values, we can use the mode (the most frequent value) or count the number of occurrences of the different possible values.

More precisely, in the framework of the preceding chapter, we define a local propositionalization function φ' as follows. Let C be a clause with $vars(C) = \{Y_1, \ldots, Y_m\}$. Let $T := val(C, e, B)$. Further, if T is not the empty set, let $T_i := \pi_i(T)$. If T is the empty set, T_i may be a tuple containing as a single component the symbol for a missing value. We assume aggregate functions to be defined for missing values. For a numeric variable $Y_i \in vars(C)$, we define

$$\varphi'(T_i) := (avg(T_i), max(T_i), min(T_i), sum(T_i)) \ , \tag{4.7}$$

where $avg(T_i)$, $max(T_i)$, $min(T_i)$, and $sum(T_i)$ compute the average, maximum, minimum, and sum of the values in T_i, respectively. For a nominal variable $Y_i \in vars(C)$, we define

$$\varphi'(T_i) := \bigoplus_{v \in domain(Y_i)} (\mid \sigma_{1=v}(T_i) \mid) \ , \tag{4.8}$$

where $domain(Y_i)$ is the ordered set of possible values for Y_i, and $\sigma_{1=v}(T_i)$ means the selection of all tuples from T_i where the single component (with index 1) has value v. Multiset cardinality can be determined with the help of the aggregate function *count*.

Again, $\bigoplus$ denotes tuple concatenation. In addition, we use the total size of the set T as a feature, determined by *count* again. All this results in the transformation function

$$\varphi(C,T) := (\mid T \mid) \bigoplus_{i=1..m} \varphi'(T_i) \ . \tag{4.9}$$

In the implementation, we apply a further restriction w.r.t. $domain(Y_i)$. A nominal variable Y_i is neglected, if its *cardinality* exceeds a user-provided threshold.

Further, argument positions that are used for foreign link definitions exclude corresponding variables from aggregation. In other words, identifiers are not used here.

A function Φ was chosen to produce attribute names for the tuples resulting from propositionalization. This function ensures unique attribute names by including information about the items used in the computation of the attribute values. These are a short name for the aggregate function applied, a name for the predicate from E or B concerned, the position/name of the argument, if applicable, and an identification of $C \in \mathcal{C}$.

4.3 An Algorithm for Propositionalization

The components discussed above in this chapter result in an algorithm which is given in Table 4.1. Step 2 of the algorithm implements the clause construction process based on foreign links, in step 2a. Also, it removes redundant clauses and thus the redundant features they would otherwise give rise to, in step 2b. For further details of the clause generation step, the interested reader is referred to the presentation by Wrobel [133]. Steps 3 to 5 implement the construction of the propositional table based on the transformation function φ defined above.

The algorithm as shown here is specific about $\mathcal{C}$, but allows for other φ than those listed in the preceding section. Further, we omit details of parameter usage (branching factor, maximum cardinality of possible value sets for nominal attributes) to keep the presentation simple.

We call our approach to propositionalization using aggregate functions RE-LAGGS, which stands for RELational AGGregationS. It can also be conveived as an homage to the idea of relative least general generalization (RLGG), which was among the early influences in ILP [99, 89], although not used here.

We illustrate the workings of the algorithm with the help of our running example, cf. Appendix D.

Example 21 *Consider tables* t, a, b, *and* c *of the running example. The first record in table* t *as an element of the set of examples E corresponds to the Prolog fact*

t(1,1,1,pos).

Analogously, Prolog facts can be written down for the entries of tables a, b, *and* c. *Further, foreign link declarations may obey the following pattern:*

link(<rel1>:<pos1>, <rel2>:<pos2>).

with "rel" for relation, and "pos" for argument position. Then, let the ordered set of foreign links $\mathcal{L}$ be

link(t:1,a:2).
link(a:1,b:2).
link(a:3,c:1).

The first definition means that a variable can be shared by a t *literal and an* a *literal that occur in a clause. That variable must be in the first argument position for the* t *literal and in the second argument position for the* a *literal. Analogous for the other foreign link definitions.*

Note the correspondence with foreign key relationships from the database schema, apart from direction. With these definitions, the following example clauses C_1, C_2, and C_3 can be generated and further processed.

Consider

$C_1 = $ t(A,B,C,D) :- a(E,A,F,G,H).

In a first step, $val(C_1, e, B)$ is determined, which is depicted in Figure 4.2. Here, we only consider body variables in order to keep the presentation simple. Each line corresponds to a tuple of values of $val(C_1, e, B)$. Body variables from C_1 are ordered here in the same way as in the clause itself.

In a second step, φ and τ are applied and result in Figure 4.3, which shows the propositionalized table of E and B with $\mathcal{C} = \{C_1\}$. Here, count means the

Table 4.1: RELAGGS algorithm

1. **Accept** as input: examples E, background knowledge B (n predicates), foreign links $\mathcal{L}$, functional dependencies $\mathcal{F}$

2. **Construct** clause set $\mathcal{C}$:

   (a) **Generate** all clauses C subject to the following restrictions:

      i. all literals $L \in C$ have variables in all argument positions

      ii. a target predicate literal serves as head

      iii. each background knowledge predicate occurs at most once

      iv. each body literal shares exactly one variable with a literal occuring earlier in the clause, according to $\mathcal{L}$

      v. each possible set of body literals is used only once to build a clause

   (b) **Eliminate** C if there is $C' = CLC''$, with $f \in \mathcal{F}$ specifying a functional dependency between $D \subseteq C$ and L

3. **Generate** a new line for $TABLE$

4. **For** all $C \in \mathcal{C}$

   (a) **Determine** $\Phi(C)$

   (b) **For** all $Att_i \in \Phi(C)$, append Att_i to $TABLE$

5. **For** all $e \in E$

   (a) **Generate** a new line for $TABLE$

   (b) **For** all $C \in \mathcal{C}$

      i. Determine $T = val(C, e, B)$

      ii. Determine $\varphi(C, T)$

      iii. For all $v \in \varphi(C, T)$ append v to $TABLE$

   (c) **Append** class value of e to $TABLE$, if applicable

6. **Output** $TABLE$

val(C₁,e,B)				
Eσ	Aσ	Fσ	Gσ	Hσ
1	1	1	10	x
2	1	1	20	y
...	...	...	...	...

Figure 4.2: The result of $val(C_1, e, B)$ for body variables

τ({C₁},E⁺,E⁻,B)								
T_id	count	avg(Gσ)	max(Gσ)	min(Gσ)	sum(Gσ)	count(Hσ=x)	count(Hσ=y)	T_cl
1	2	15	20	10	30	1	1	pos
...	...	...	...	...	...	...	...	...

Figure 4.3: The propositional table based on C_1, i.e. $\tau(\{C_1\}, E^+, E^-, B)$

size of $val(C_1, e, B)$, while count(X=x) means the size of a subset of $val(C_1, e, B)$ where the attribute corresponding to variable X takes on value x.

Let C_1 as above,
$C_2 = \texttt{t(A,B,C,D) :- a(E,A,F,G,H), c(F,I,J).}$
Let us assume, the set of functional dependencies $\mathcal{F}$ contains a description of such a dependency between a and c, i.e.

$\{\texttt{a(\_,\_,F,\_,\_)}\} \rhd \texttt{c(F,\_,\_)}.$

Then, $val(C_2, e, B)$ produces tuples as depicted in Figure 4.4. The result of $val(C_2, e, B)$ differs from $val(C_1, e, B)$ only in the additional columns for I and J. Especially, the columns for G and H are the same in both tables such that any local aggregate function applied here would not yield different results for $val(C_1, e, B)$ and $val(C_2, e, B)$. Hence, we can decide to not consider C_1.

val(C₂,e,B)						
Eσ	Aσ	Fσ	Gσ	Hσ	Iσ	Jσ
1	1	1	10	x	1.1	xx
2	1	1	20	y	1.1	xx
...	...	...	...	...	...	...

Figure 4.4: The result of $val(C_2, e, B)$ for body variables

Let now C_2 as above,
$C_3 = \texttt{t(A,B,C,D) :- a(E,A,F,G,H), b(K,E,L,M).}$
For this clause, the functional dependency given above does not apply. Figure 4.5 shows $val(C_3, e, B)$. Here, there are differences with respect to the columns for G

and H of $val(C_2, e, B)$ and $val(C_3, e, B)$. This way, there can be different aggregates as well. For example, the average of G for $val(C_2, e, B)$ is 15, while it is 16.6 for $val(C_3, e, B)$. This can be viewed as weighting the property G of an item a in the light of the number of related items b. This illustrates why our algorithm will consider both C_2 and C_3 for the computation of the final propositionalized table.

val(C_3,e,B)							
Eσ	Aσ	Fσ	Gσ	Hσ	Kσ	Lσ	Mσ
1	1	1	10	x	1	100	X
2	1	1	20	y	2	200	X
2	1	1	20	y	3	300	Y
...	...	...	...	...	...	...	...

Figure 4.5: The result of $val(C_3, e, B)$ for body variables

The weighting effect may also occur for head variables.

Note that aggregation can be seen as an operator orthogonal to other operators typical for relational database queries: selection, projection, join, and also other arithmetic operations on single relations as used for conventional feature construction. This view enables a simpler analysis of algorithms that use aggregation, among others w.r.t. their complexity, and also a simpler design of new algorithms of this kind such as RELAGGS.

4.4 Related Work

In this section, we review two approaches that also use aggregate functions for propositionalization. The first approach is called ROLLUP and was developed and presented by Knobbe and colleagues [54, 53]. Relational concept classes were presented by Perlich and colleagues [96]. We again take the view of our framework for the analysis of these two approaches and systems, respectively. We also compare with relevant aspects of RELAGGS.

4.4.1 ROLLUP

The Approach of ROLLUP

ROLLUP [54, 53] considers a relational database as a graph — for central parts of the algorithm as an undirected graph — with relations as nodes and foreign key relationships as edges. It performs a depth-first search in this graph up to a certain, user-defined depth d. On encountering a table s at a current depth $d_{cur} \leq d$, two cases are differentiated.

First, if there is a one-to-many relationship between tables r and s, with r at depth $d_{cur} - 1$ via which s was reached, then s is summarized with the help of aggregate functions with respect to the foreign key attribute pointing to the primary key of r. The summary features are then added to r.

Second, if there is a many-to-one relationship between r and s, the attributes of s can be added to r without the necessity for summarizations. This process is executed, starting with $d_{cur} = d$, then recursively with decreasing values for d_{cur} until summary features of all tables up to a distance d are added to the target table.

In the framework presented above, ROLLUP can be described in the following way.

A set of clauses *Base* is defined that will serve as a basis for sets $\mathcal{C}$ to be used within the framework described above:

$$Base := \{p(X, \ldots) : -q_1(Y_1, \ldots), \ldots, q_k(Y_k, \ldots) \quad | \quad 1 \leq k \leq d;$$
$$p(X, \ldots, Y_1, \ldots) \text{ or}$$
$$q_1(Y_1, \ldots, X, \ldots);$$
$$\forall q_i, q_{i+1}(1 \leq i \leq k - 1) :$$
$$q_i(Y_i, \ldots, Y_{i+1}, \ldots) \text{ or}$$
$$q_{i+1}(Y_{i+1}, \ldots, Y_i, \ldots)\}$$

In other words, two neighboring literals share a variable corresponding to the foreign key relationship of the relations concerned. All these clauses in *Base* are most general in the sense that all argument positions are filled with variables. These clauses can be constructed with a depth-first search algorithm in analogy to the character of ROLLUP.

In the following, we differentiate between two variants of ROLLUP that arise from our interpretations of the algorithm's description. First, there is a minimalist variant, which uses clauses of length up to d. There may be shorter clauses in use because literals of a predicate should occur only once in a clause. Second, there is a maximalist variant, which uses clauses of exactly length d only, possibly using more than one literal of a predicate.

Example 22 *For the running example and $d = 1$, Base consists of:*

1. *$t(T,F,G,Class)$:- $a(A,T,C,An,Ac)$.*

2. *$t(T,F,G,Class)$:- $d(D,T,E,Dn,Dc)$.*

3. *$t(T,F,G,Class)$:- $f(F,F2,E,Fn,Fc)$.*

4. *$t(T,F,G,Class)$:- $g(G,Gn,Gc)$.*

For $d = 2$, it consists of the following clauses, assuming a minimalist variant of ROLLUP*:*

1. *t(T,F,G,Class) :- a(A,T,C,An,Ac), b(B,A,Bn,Bc).*

2. *t(T,F,G,Class) :- a(A,T,C,An,Ac), c(C,Cn,Cc).*

3. *t(T,F,G,Class) :- d(D,T,E,Dn,Dc), e(E,En,Ec).*

4. *t(T,F,G,Class) :- f(F,F2,E,Fn,Fc), e(E,En,Ec).*

5. *t(T,F,G,Class) :- g(G,Gn,Gc).*

For $d = 3$, again assuming a minimalist variant:

1. *t(T,F,G,Class) :- a(A,T,C,An,Ac), b(B,A,Bn,Bc).*

2. *t(T,F,G,Class) :- a(A,T,C,An,Ac), c(C,Cn,Cc).*

3. *t(T,F,G,Class) :- d(D,T,E,Dn,Dc), e(E,En,Ec), f(F,F2,E,Fn,Fc).*

4. *t(T,F,G,Class) :- f(F,F2,E,Fn,Fc), e(E,En,Ec), d(D,T,E,Dn,Dc).*

5. *t(T,F,G,Class) :- g(G,Gn,Gc).*

For $d = 2$ and a maximalist variant of ROLLUP*, all clauses in Base would have two literals in the body such that there are the following clauses, the last clause replacing the last one given above for $d = 2$ and the minimalist variant:*

- *t(T,F,G,Class) :- a(A,T,C,An,Ac), t(T,F,G,Class).*

- *...*

- *t(T,F,G,Class) :- g(G,Gn,Gc), t(T,F,G,Class).*

The algorithm as originally presented by Knobbe and colleagues [54] in its more formal variant indicates this maximalistic variant, while the text also speaks of "leaf(s) in the graph" as end points for recursive search, which allows the minimalist interpretation.

Example 23 *Note that clauses of the pattern* t :- g, t. *can lead to interesting results because of the many-to-one relationship between* t *and* g. *Here, for a specific example from* t, *information about other examples from* t *will be aggregated that have a relationship with the same tuple of* g.

Back to the minimalist case, *Base* is partitioned into subsets $Base_i$ (this partitioning would not be necessary for the maximalist variant since all clauses in *Base* are of the same length d there; the other steps remain the same):

$$Base_i := \{C = p(X, \ldots) : -q_1(Y_1, \ldots), \ldots, q_k(Y_k, \ldots) \mid C \in Base; k = i\} \quad (4.10)$$

For the running example and $d = 2$, $Base_2$ consists of the first four clauses from *Base* as provided above, $Base_1$ consists of the last clause.

Beginning with $i = d$, each such set $Base_i$ is partitioned into subsets $Base_{ij}$:

$$Base_{ij} := \{C = p(X, \ldots) : -q_1(Y_1, \ldots), \ldots, q_k(Y_k, \ldots) \mid C \in Base_i;$$
$$q_1, \ldots, q_{k-1} \ fixed\}$$

In other words, clauses in each set $Base_{ij}$ differ in their last literal only.

Example 24 *For the running example, we arrive at three clause sets $Base_{2j}$, one of those, say $Base_{21}$, made up of*

1. *t(T,F,G,Class) :- a(A,T,C,An,Ac), b(B,A,Bn,Bc).*

2. *t(T,F,G,Class) :- a(A,T,C,An,Ac), c(C,Cn,Cc).*

The other two subsets have only one element each.

For members of such a set $Base_{ij}$, the last two literals are used to construct new clauses where the first literal forms the head and the second the body. These new clauses form clause sets A_{ij}.

Example 25 *For the running example, the subset $Base_{21}$ given above results in new clauses to form a clause set A_{21}, where a takes over the role of a temporary target predicate:*

1. *a(A,T,C,An,Ac) :- b(B,A,Bn,Bc).*

2. *a(A,T,C,An,Ac) :- c(C,Cn,Cc).*

A clause set A_{ij} can now be used as a clause set $\mathcal{C}$ as presented in the framework above, apart from the very last step of adding in the class attribute. This is only possible in case the head literal corresponds to the target relation. The result of this propositionalization is added to the background knowledge in an appropriate way. That means, for instance, background knowledge is expanded by computed tuple values as arguments of a new predicate the name of which could be derived from the predicate names of clauses in A_{ij}.

The clauses in a subset $Base_{ij}$ are furthermore used to construct a new clause built from the original literals up to the last two. Those last two are replaced by a literal that stands for the result of the computations within the framework with A_{ij} as $\mathcal{C}$. This newly constructed clause is added to $Base_{i-1}$.

Example 26 *For the running example, this produces as a new member for Base$_1$:*

- $t(T,F,G,Class)$:- $a\_b\_c(A,T,C,An,Ac,...)$.

Here, the dots represent summary features originating from b and c.

Finally, the process is repeated with the step of the construction of $Base_{i-1,j}$. After d such loops, the head literal of each clause in the single remaining set of clauses $A_{1,1}$ used as C corresponds to the target predicate and the algorithm finishes after the corresponding last propositionalization, now with adding in class values.

Relevant aspects of RELAGGS

Consider again Figure 4.1 above. Acyclicity in such graphs allows RELAGGS [71] to have no parameter for depth as ROLLUP. The set of clauses C for background knowledge with n different predicates is defined here as:

$$C := \{p(X,....) : -q_1(Y_1,...,),...,q_k(Y_k,...) \mid 1 \leq k \leq n;$$
$$\forall q_i, q_j \ with \ 0 \leq i \leq k-1,$$
$$i < j, p = q_0 : q_i <> q_j;$$
$$q_i(Y_i,...,Y_j,...) \ or$$
$$q_j(Y_j,...,Y_i,...);$$
$$only \ one \ permutation \ per$$
$$possible \ set \ of \ body \ literals\}$$

In other words, C consists of all clauses with up to n body literals of different predicates, with each body literal sharing one variable with a literal anywhere to its left in the clause.

Example 27 *For the running example, RELAGGS would determine the following clauses with one literal in the body for the set of clauses C:*

1. $t(T,F,G,Class)$:- $a(A,T,C,An,Ac)$.

2. $t(T,F,G,Class)$:- $d(D,T,E,Dn,Dc)$.

3. $t(T,F,G,Class)$:- $f(F,F2,E,Fn,Fc)$.

4. $t(T,F,G,Class)$:- $g(G,Gn,Gc)$.

Also, the following clauses with two literals in the body, the first of which is an a literal, would be added to C:

- $t(T,F,G,Class)$:- $a(A,T,C,An,Ac)$, $b(B,A,Bn,Bc)$.

- $t(T,F,G,Class)$:- $a(A,T,C,An,Ac)$, $c(C,Cn,Cc)$.

- $t(T,F,G,Class)$:- $a(A,T,C,An,Ac)$, $d(D,T,E,Dn,Dc)$.

- $t(T,F,G,Class)$:- $a(A,T,C,An,Ac)$, $f(F,F2,E,Fn,Fc)$

- $t(T,F,G,Class)$:- $a(A,T,C,An,Ac)$, $g(G,Gn,Gc)$.

Then come other two-literal clauses and clauses with more than two literals in the body. From the following three-literal clauses, only the first is chosen because of the condition on permutations:

- $t(T,F,G,Class)$:- $a(A,T,C,An,Ac)$, $b(B,A,Bn,Bc)$, $c(C,Cn,Cc)$.

- $t(T,F,G,Class)$:- $a(A,T,C,An,Ac)$, $c(C,Cn,Cc)$, $b(B,A,Bn,Bc)$.

The largest clause for $\mathcal{C}$ is the following:

- $t(T,F,G,Class)$:- $a(A,T,C,An,Ac)$, $b(B,A,Bn,Bc)$, $c(C,Cn,Cc)$, $d(D,T,E,Dn,Dc)$, $e(E,En,Ec)$, $f(F,F2,E,Fn,Fc)$, $g(G,Gn,Gc)$.

Many of the clauses in $\mathcal{C}$ can be discarded based on functional dependencies without losing information when applying local aggregate functions. Furthermore, with a parameter *branching factor* set to 0, only paths in the graph are considered for clause construction, and no more complex subgraphs. For instance, this would discard the last three clauses with two literals in the body the first of which is an a literal above.

Example 28 *An adequately reduced set $\mathcal{C}$ would consist of the following clauses, sorted first by length, then lexicographically considering predicate names:*

1. $t(T,F,G,Class)$:- $g(G,Gn,Gc)$.

2. $t(T,F,G,Class)$:- $a(A,T,C,An,Ac)$, $b(B,A,Bn,Bc)$.

3. $t(T,F,G,Class)$:- $a(A,T,C,An,Ac)$, $c(C,Cn,Cc)$.

4. $t(T,F,G,Class)$:- $d(D,T,E,Dn,Dc)$, $e(E,En,Ec)$.

5. $t(T,F,G,Class)$:- $f(F,F2,E,Fn,Fc)$, $e(E,En,Ec)$.

This reduced set $\mathcal{C}$ can be used within the framework as such.

To illustrate the reduction, we give the following examples. A clause with body literals for a, b, *and* c *was dropped because of the zero branching factor. Clauses with just a* d *literal or an* f *literal in the body were dropped because of the functional dependencies between* d *and* e *and between* f *and* e, *respectively.*

Comparison of RollUp **and** Relaggs

Usability Here, we consider parameters that can be set by the user.

For RollUp, the user has to specify the parameter depth d. With increasing values for d, relations more distant from the target table can thus be included in the analysis. The largest distance between the target table and another relation in the schema of the relational database may support a decision about a largest useful value for d. There may arise difficulties with the maximalist variant of RollUp though, cf. remarks on complexity below.

For Relaggs, the user has to specify the foreign links. As a starting point, the schema of the relational database, especially the foreign key relationships therein, is of help to the user here. Nevertheless, there are degrees of freedom for the construction of foreign links. First, in the common case of circles in the graph induced by the relational database, these have to be resolved. Second, other links not corresponding to foreign key relationships may be defined.

Further, functional dependencies may be specified by the user based on an investigation of many-to-one relationships according to the database schema. Last not least, the user may specify the restrictions of a braching factor and of maximum cardinalities of the sets of possible values for nominal attributes to be considered for propositionalization.

For an evaluation of the situation, we see that RollUp demands for less preparatory work by the user than Relaggs. However, our impression from empirical work is that this preparatory work is useful, e. g. to avoid explosive behavior of $\mathcal{C}$'s cardinality.

Complexity This paragraph considers numbers of clauses produced for propositionalization, numbers of tuples in join results, and numbers of features constructed.

For RollUp, the number of clauses in *Base* can be restricted by the value of search depth d. With a maximalist variant, however, there can be an exponential growth of the number of those clauses with increasing d.

The depth-first algorithm avoids complexity problems with join results. It computes joins of at most two tables. Here, the number of tuples in any single join result is not larger than the number of tuples in the larger one of the two relations to be joined.

The number of features produced by RollUp is exponential in d. For instance, if 4 aggregate functions *avg*, *max*, *min*, and *sum* would be applied to numeric attributes, such a numeric attribute in a table at distance d from the target table would result in $4^{(d/2)}$ summary features in the propositionalization result because of repeated aggregation. This assumes an average case of half the relationships on a path from the target relation to the farthest non-target relation to be one-to-many relationships, and the others many-to-one relationships.

With no parameter for the restriction of the analysis to nominal attributes with up to a certain number of possible values, there is another danger for RollUp to further increase the number of resulting features enormously.

For Relaggs, the number of clauses in $\mathcal{C}$ can grow exponentially with the number of different relations, considering bodies of clauses as arbitrary subsets of literals from the set of all possible literals as provided by the background knowledge.

Also, joins involving not directly related tables can produce results larger than any single original table involved. This case is illustrated by the following example.

Example 29 *For the running example, such a join is represented by*

  1. t(T,F,G,Class) :- a(A,T,C,An,Ac), d(D,T,E,Dn,Dc).

In the result, each tuple for a *is combined with each tuple for* d, *as long as they have the same value for variable T.*

These effects, for both clause numbers and join result sizes, are avoided by setting the parameter branching factor to value 0. Moreover, the information loss from this setting can be remedied by computations from aggregation results produced with the help of other clauses, as shown in the following example.

Example 30 *For the running example, the following two clauses (or clauses producing identical columns from* a *and* d*) would be included in* $\mathcal{C}$ *with branching factor set to 0:*

  1. t(T,F,G,Class) :- a(A,T,C,An,Ac).

  2. t(T,F,G,Class) :- d(D,T,E,Dn,Dc).

Since the results of a join including a *and* d *would just produce multiples of entries as in these two joins, those multiples can be produced after propositionalization based on counts and other aggregation results, if needed.*

The number of features is not as critical as it is for RollUp. Once joins are computed, it grows linearly with the number of numeric attributes and the number of possible values of nominal attributes, as long as the setting of the cardinality parameter allows to consider the latter at all.

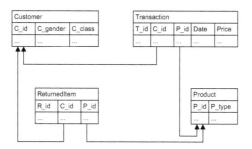

Figure 4.6: A relational database schema [96] (arrows represent foreign key relationships)

Features In the following, we consider the set of features produced under the different approaches, under a semantic perspective.

There are overlaps between the ROLLUP and RELAGGS clauses for *Base* and *C*, respectively. However, due to the different usage of those clauses, the final results are different.

For instance, RELAGGS produces summary features for *a* tuples that are weighted by related tuples in *b*, which is not the case with ROLLUP. On the other hand, ROLLUP produces many more summary features for *b* because of repeated summarization, cf. subsection on complexity above. The potentials for expressiveness of those many features should be further investigated. Some aspects are considered in this chapter's section on our experimental work below.

Note that there are potential differences by the usage of different aggregate functions as well. Originally, however, both ROLLUP and RELAGGS used the same set of functions in the same way, influenced by the SQL standard.

4.4.2 Relational Concept Classes

Ideas and Implementations for Relational Concept Classes

Perlich and Provost [96] provide an example relational database for illustrative purposes that is depicted in Fig. 4.6 in a form analogous to that of our running example. In the original paper, arrows are used differently, unfortunately without explanation. In the following, we will also analyze some of the examples presented by the authors of that paper that refer to this database.

Aggregation Perlich and Provost [97, 96] adopt the view that a relational concept is a function Φ that includes as an argument an example from the target relation t with its target value y and as another argument a fixed number of aggregates of objects that are related to the target case through keys, as a result of a complex aggregation function Ψ applied to the background knowledge RDB, i. e. all relations in the database except t:

$$y = \Phi(t, \Psi(RDB)) \tag{4.11}$$

Φ corresponds in our framework to the application of a result from conventional data mining, i. e. a propositional model, to the tuple resulting from the concatenation of tuple t with that from $\Psi(RDB)$.

Ψ seems to be a concept similar to concatenating the propositionalization function φ results in our framework, cf. function *prop* there. However, details as contained in our definition of φ, viz. using clauses as queries to the relational database and their results per target object, are not provided by the authors.

Ψ is called an "aggregation function" by Perlich and Provost [96]. This notion can be misleading, though, as we will explain below. We see aggregate functions as a means within a propositionalization function, but do not identify the propositionalization function with an aggregate function.

Perlich and Provost [96], however, differentiate between

Simple aggregation: a mapping from a bag of zero or more atomic values to a categorical or numerical value (general examples: mean for a bag of numeric values, mode for a bag of categorical values, counts of specific values for a bag of categorical values, ...)

Multi-dimensional aggregation: mapping from a bag of feature vectors describing objects to a categorical or numerical value (example A: total amount spent over the last two weeks; example B: Boolean value [as possibly both categorical and numerical] for a bag of transactions to describe if a customer is buying increasingly more-expensive products)

Multi-type aggregation: mapping from two or more bags of feature vectors describing objects to a categorical or numerical value (example C: total value of products a customer has returned, example D: most recent date on which a customer bought a product that was commonly returned before)

From the point of view of our framework, both "multi-dimensional aggregation" and "multi-type aggregation" can be expressed using "simple aggregation" after appropriate selections from the database:

Example A: first select the amounts spent over the last two weeks, then compute the value for aggregate function *sum* for the resulting bag of values

Example B: first select identifiers of transactions of a customer such that there is a transaction with a later date and lower price, then *count* the values in the result and map 0 to true, other values to false

Example C: first select identifiers of products from ReturnedItems for a customer, then the prices for these products for that customer from Transactions, finally *sum* those prices

Example D: first select ids of products from ReturnedItems that were commonly returned (using *count*), then select dates on which a customer bought those products, finally determine *max* of those dates

The differentiation of aggregate functions as done by Perlich and Provost [96] seems not to clarify the situation, especially because it deviates from the widespread concept of aggregate functions in the database area corresponding to the concept of "simple aggregation" here. We see the simple aggregate operators as favorable not only with respect to comprehensibility, but also as building blocks to be combined with other operators for joins, selections, projections, feature construction within one relation, etc.

Actually, there seem to be open issues in the presentation by Perlich and Provost [96] that maybe arise from their over-complicated view at aggregation: all three of their types of aggregation output just one value, more clearly to be seen in [97] than in [96], while $\Psi(RDB)$ in the formula given above is supposed to return a tuple of aggregates.

Note that in our framework as presented above, there can be other relationships between objects than those established by foreign key relationships.

A Hierarchy of Relational Concept Classes Based on their definitions of aggregation functions, Perlich and Provost present a hierarchy of relational concept classes. Here, a concept class M_2 is more complex than a concept class M_1 if any concept δ in M_1 can be expressed in M_2 and there are concepts in M_2 that cannot be expressed in M_1.

While Perlich and Provost [97] at first defined 8 concept classes, these were later condensed into 5 [96]. These are presented here in terms of our framework, in the original order of growing "complexity of the most complex aggregation used" [96]. We also keep the names for those classes here:

i) Propositional Here, clauses for $\mathcal{C}$ are allowed that take the following form:

- p(X,...,Y,...) :- q(Y,_,...,Z1,_,...,Z2,_,...).

Such a clause exploits a one-to-one or many-to-one relationship between p and q.

This largely corresponds to the restriction to determinate clauses as used for DINUS, there without the restriction to function-free clauses. For each target object described by a p tuple, there is at most one q tuple that can be concatenated to the p tuple. By the anonymous variables, we indicate that Perlich and

Provost suggest the opportunity for projections here, resulting in only specific components of a q tuple to form a new tuple that is concatenated to the p tuple. This projection could also be achieved by post-processing of the propositionalized table, e. g. with conventional feature selectors.

As examples, Perlich and Provost mention the common case where a customer table can be enriched with data from a demographics table.

Example 31 *For the running example, this allows for the usage of the following* $\mathcal{C}$:

1. *$t(T,F,G,Class)$:- $f(F,\_,E,Fn,\_)$.*

2. *$t(T,F,G,Class)$:- $g(G,Gn,Gc)$.*

There are many-to-one relationships from the target relation to both f *and* g, *but not to any other tables in the database.*

ii) Independent Attributes   This is the least complex relational concept class, where a one-to-many relationship between p and q should be exploited. Clauses for $\mathcal{C}$ take the following form:

- $p(X,...)$:- $q(\_,X,\_,...,Z,\_,...$).

A single projected attribute Z is treated here by "simple aggregation".

An example given by Perlich and Provost [96] is "average price of products bought" by a customer.

A further interesting example provided by the authors is "the proportion of products returned by the customer". The authors state that this would demand for one *count* on table Transaction and another *count* on table ReturnedItems. Then, Φ would compute the proportion. This last step corresponds to conventional feature construction.

Example 32 *For the running example, this concept class allows for the usage of the following* $\mathcal{C}$:

1. *$t(T,F,G,Class)$:- $a(\_,T,\_,An,\_)$.*

2. *$t(T,F,G,Class)$:- $a(\_,T,\_,\_,Ac)$.*

3. *$t(T,F,G,Class)$:- $d(\_,T,\_,Dn,\_)$.*

4. *$t(T,F,G,Class)$:- $d(\_,T,\_,\_,Dc)$.*

There are direct one-to-many relationships from the target relation to both a *and* d, *but not to any other tables in the database.*

Note that key attributes are not included in the aggregation here (the first argument of the body literals is always an anonymous variable) and for the following concept classes. However, this may be to rigid, cf. Section 5.4.

iii) Dependent Attributes within one Table   Here, aggregation is performed for subbags of those used in the concept class before. These subbags are achieved by specific selection conditions:

- p(X,...) :- q(_,X,_,...,Z,_,...,Cond,_,...), Cond = <value>.

Instead of =, there might also be other relational operators such as >, ≥ etc. for numerical variables.

Examples by Perlich and Provost are "the number of products bought on December 22nd" by a customer and, as given above, "slope of price over time", i.e. the question if the customer is buying increasingly more-expensive products.

Example 33 *For the running example, $\mathcal{C}$ consists of clauses such as*

1. *t(T,F,G,Class) :- a(_,T,_,An,x).*

2. *t(T,F,G,Class) :- a(_,T,_,An,y).*

3. *t(T,F,G,Class) :- a(_,T,_,Cond,Ac), Cond > 15.*

4. *...*

iv) Dependent Attributes across Tables   The general form of clauses for $\mathcal{C}$ here is:

- p(X,...) :- q(_,X,_,...,Z1,_,...,Z2,_,...), r(_,X,_,...,Z3,_,...,Z4,_,...).

As an example, Perlich and Provost give "the total amount spent on items returned" by a customer. This is actually a special case because Transaction and ReturnedItems have foreign key attributes for both product identifiers and customer identifiers. So, the corresponding clause would look like:

- customer(C,...) :- returned(_,C,P), transaction(_,C,P,_,Price_).

Note the restrictions of the join of ReturnedItems and Transaction by two foreign key conditions.

In the general case, where q and r share only the key attribute with p, the aggregation results can be computed from the aggregated single joins between p and q and between p and r, respectively, with the help of conventional feature construction.

Example 34 *For the running example, $\mathcal{C}$ would contain clauses such as the following:*

- *t(T,F,G,Class) :- a(_,T,_,An,Ac), d(_,T,_,Dn,_).*

v) Global Graph Features   Perlich and Provost state that "multi-type aggregation" has to be applied here to the transitive closure over a set of possible joins. Such a global concept could for instance be a function of customer reputation. This may require the construction of an adjacency matrix and the calculation of its Eigenvalues and Eigenvectors.

This class of relational concepts needs further investigation. So far, the presentation in [96] seems underspecified.

Between Levels   Perlich and Provost further evaluate their hierarchy as "coarse". At sublevels, they see, among others, the usage of autocorrelation with the help of joins back to the target relation.

Remarks   The definitions provided by Perlich and Provost use only relations that share a key variable with the target relation. They state that the hierarchy can be extended in a straightforward way to cases of further distant relations. This seems to be the case for the example provided that encompasses a chain of joins along one-to-many relationships. It seems also intuitive for a chain of joins along many-to-one relationships.

However, this deals not yet with more complex situations of sequences of joins with both one-to-many and many-to-one relationships involved, cf. our concept of functional dependencies and its exploitation. It neither treats cases of joins not along paths in the graph induced by the relational database, cf. our comments on concept class iv above.

The hierarchy seems to be equivalent to restricting $\mathcal{C}$ in different ways. Restrictions such as these are necessary to achieve efficient implementations of propositionalization.

New Usage of Aggregate Functions   For their paper [96], the authors consider predictive relational learning tasks, i. e. tasks with a target table within a relational database containing a target variable, either numeric for regression or categorical for classification. This circumstance is relevant for the new usage of aggregate functions as presented by Perlich and Provost [96], since it deals with target-dependent aggregation.

Note that our framework presented above could also be used for descriptive relational learning tasks by just leaving out the final step of adding in the class attribute in cases where there is none available.

The new kind of propositionalization functions by Perlich and Provost applies to their concept class ii and to categorical attributes of the non-target relations.

Unfortunatly, the description of queries equivalent to clauses in $\mathcal{C}$ in our framework is rather short [96]. The same applies to the real-life business database that they use for their experiments. For the latter, foreign key relationships remain blurred.

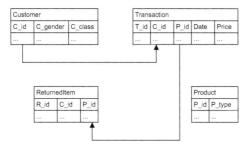

Figure 4.7: A relational database schema [96] (arrows represent user-defined foreign links)

For categorical attributes, several vectors are computed. These are case vectors CV that contain counts of possible values per target example, reference vectors RV that contain especially counts of possible values across all positive examples and across all negative examples, further so-called variance vectors.

The authors investigate different extracts from CVs. For instance, they only keep the counts of possible values that occur most often across positive examples and those that occur most often across negative examples. Another opportunity is to keep those counts, where the counts for possible values across positives differ the most from those across negatives.

Further, distances between CVs and RVs are used to produce further features, using different opportunities to compute vector distances.

Results show that features of increasing complexity have increasing predictive power in the domain investigated. However, there are no details about runtimes given.

Relevant aspects of RELAGGS

Here, we point to some problems of RELAGGS [71] with the RCC example database, and we describe where RELAGGS clauses can be found in the RCC hierarchy.

Fig. 4.7 depicts the example database of Perlich and Provost with just two foreign links.

For the relational concept class iv, Perlich and Provost gave the example of "the total price of products returned by a customer". Using the foreign links as defined in the figure, there can be a clause $C \in \mathcal{C}$:

- customer(C,Gender,Class) :- transaction(T,C,P,Date,Price), returnedItem(R,C2,P).

Since foreign links as used by RELAGGS allow for only one variable to be shared between a pair of literals there cannot be variable C in the last literal.

This means, that for each product bought by a certain customer, information about returns of this product will be included across all customers.

It would not help to declare a different foreign link, say from Transaction.C_id to ReturnedItems.C_id: in this case, every transaction record for a certain customer is joined with all records on returned items of this customer. So, here the bias for RELAGGS clauses excludes a relational concept.

However, the database schema itself seems to be problematic. Instead of identifiers for customers and products, those for transactions would have been more appropriate in the ReturnedItems table. With this new schema, RELAGGS would have no problems.

Another interesting example provided by Perlich and Provost, in the context of statements on the large expressive power of ILP, corresponds to the following:

- customer(C,Gender,Class) :- transaction(T,C,P,Date,Price),
  returnedItem(R,C2,P), transaction(T2,C2,P,Date2,Price2), date2 $\geq$ 2001.

This identifies customers who bought a product that was returned by another customer who bought it after 2001. The RELAGGS bias excludes a clause such as this, because it does not allow for multiple occurrences of literals of the same predicate in a clause C.

Another problem for the RELAGGS bias is posed by autocorrelation. As Perlich and Provost point out, this can be treated by linking back to the target relation. However, the RELAGGS bias does not allow for a target literal in the clause body. Moreover, this would introduce circles in the graph induced by the database. Thus, a parameter for search depth like d for RollUp [54] or a similar parameter for the RCC-based system [96] would be necessary.

Actually, some of the deficiencies can be remedied by constructing further tables, for instance, in the case of autocorrelation, by producing copies of the target relation and possibly further relations, as was already tried successfully in a biological domain [22].

Finally, which concept class do RELAGGS clauses correspond to? Class i is completely covered, also class ii, if post-processing aggregates is considered a subsequent step. RELAGGS further covers parts of class iv, although just those that could be replaced by conventional feature construction from results of clauses for classes i and ii. Other parts of class iv are not covered, cf. the first example in this section above. Class iii is also not covered here, but partly by extensions, cf. the following chapter.

Comparison of RCC and RELAGGS

Since the description of the system based on RCC and the data used [96] is not detailed enough, we can not yet compare the sets of clauses used with those of RELAGGS. This situation was not improved with a dissertation overview provided by Perlich [95]. The two database schemas used there are small, with three tables each, although the structure of the second example — a citation graph from the machine learning community — allows for interesting considerations.

As for the number of features constructed, Perlich and Provost restrict this figure for categorical attributes by considering not all possible values but only selected values. The selection of these values is based on counting their occurrences across all examples, across positive examples, and across negative examples in so-called reference vectors. Then the values that occur most often under the specific conditions have to be determined. Only for those values, counts per example are used for the propositionalization result.

It is not obvious if the effort of the conditioned counting pays off compared to the RELAGGS approach of counting the occurrences of all possible values per example. There could be savings if the computation of reference vectors leads to counting only a small subset of the possible values.

However, even within the RCC-based approach, the occurrences of all possible values per example are counted and stored in so-called case vectors for the computation of distances to the reference vectors, among others.

Thus, the determination of most frequent values seems like a method for feature selection within the process of propositionalization. First, this may be costly. Second, restricting the attention to the n most frequent values may also be responsible for relevant information loss. Also, n would be another parameter to be set by the user, which is negative for ease of use.

Attributes representing distances of case vectors and reference vectors, including difference vectors for reference vectors conditioned by positive and negative examples, respectively, are not present in RELAGGS. Perlich and Provost report that they contributed to good learning results.

Overall, RCC is an interesting point of comparison for our work although the presentation by Perlich and Provost was not detailed enough so far to allow for a more precise analysis than that provided here. We expect that Perlich's dissertation will give more details.

4.5 Empirical Evaluation

4.5.1 Objectives

With a series of experiments, we demonstrate properties of the basic variant of RELAGGS as presented in this chapter. We show the 3E characteristics for our approach. This happens in relation to other systems that are suited for relational learning. RELAGGS in combination with propositional learners is compared to systems that learn directly from the relational data as well as to systems that implement traditional approaches to propositionalization.

In more detail, RELAGGS is mainly used in combination with the decision tree learner J48 as implemented in the WEKA machine learning environment [132], following many ideas of the well-known learning system C4.5 [104]. On some occasions, we also use SMO, the WEKA implementation of a support vector machine learner.

As direct learners from relational data, i. e. ILP systems in the narrow sense, we choose FOIL, PROGOL, and TILDE. This choice is motivated by the prominent status that these systems have gained in ILP. Further, they represent different approaches to relational learning and different stages of the ILP developments with TILDE as one of the most modern ILP systems.

The first of the other propositionalization systems used in our experiments is a variant of DINUS, which excludes function-free hypotheses. That means, values of relations reachable via many-to-one relationships from the target relation are used as such for the propositionalization result table.

The second of the other propositionalization systems is RSD as an implementation of the extended LINUS approach, which can also deal with indeterminate background knowledge.

Both propositionalizers are used with the same propositional learners as RELAGGS, i. e. mainly J48. The intention of our choice of these two traditional systems for propositionalization is to include two systems of different complexity into our investigations.

In the following, we present our working hypotheses (WH) for this section.

WH1A Our working hypothesis 1A is that ILP learners have better opportunities to reach high quality models, i. e. with best accuracies on the spectrum of relational learning tasks.

WH1B Also, we assume that models achieved with ILP learners have lower complexity than those resulting from the more indirect learning by propositionalization, where relational aspects of models have to be simulated with maybe numerous simpler features.

WH1C However, the inherent complexity of the ILP learners endangers them with inefficiency, especially in comparison to RELAGGS.

WH2A RELAGGS has advantages w. r. t. effectivity compared to traditional approaches to propositionalization because of its treatment of non-determinate background knowledge in a data type specific way, especially for numeric data.

WH2B Model complexity will be better for DINUS and worse for RSD, again because of the inherent simplicity / complexity of the approaches.

WH2C The same as assumed by WH2B applies to efficiency, analogously.

WH3A In a subseries of experiments, we compare to another approach to propositionalization using aggregation, viz. ROLLUP. (We cannot use an RCC system here, since it remains unclear how this system should work for more deeply structured database schemas.) Our working hypotheses for the comparison with ROLLUP is that its style of multiple aggregation scales not well.

WH3B Further, ROLLUP does presumably not produce better features. Thus, we expect about the same performance in terms of predictive accuracy and model complexity as for RELAGGS.

WH4 Another objective of our empirical evaluation is to find out if learners are really better suited to the scenario of propositionalization that can cope with a large number of possibly only moderately relevant features. This should be the case for support vector machines.

4.5.2 Material

As material for our experiments, the central relevance is put on the relational data sets and the learning tasks defined on those data.

Overall, the choice of learning tasks was motivated by the attempt to cover

- several orders of magnitude in the size of the data sets

- several domains with different characteristics such as predominant nominal descriptions or predominant numeric data

- different learning situations such as distributions of class values or learning success in general

Another criterion for our choice of data sets was availability, for obvious reasons. Here, it must be said that it would be desirable to have a larger pool of relational data sets originating from real-life databases for public access, see also Appendix B.

In order to allow for a unified treatment of learning tasks including good opportunities for the evaluation of the learning results, we restricted our attention to two-class problems, i.e. concept learning. Details about the data sets and learning tasks can be found in Appendix B. Here, we provide short descriptions to illustrate the points made above in this subsection.

Table 4.2 shows an overview of the data sets and learning tasks. The first column provides the names that we use for the learning tasks. Those names were derived from the names of the target relations and attributes. The second column indicates the domain where the data originate from. After that, we provide numbers of relations and values. The latter numbers are the products of

Table 4.2: Overview of the learning tasks (rels. — relations, vals. — values, exms. — examples, min. class — minority class)

Target	Domain	# Rels.	# Vals.	# Exms.	% Min. class
Trains20.bound	Artificial	3	796	20	50.0
KRK.illegal		2	340,000	20,000	33.0
Muta042.active	Biology/	17	59,134	42	31.0
Muta188.active	Chemistry	17	59,426	188	33.5
Partner.class	Insurance	8	4,355,315	13,322	19.5
Household.class		8	2,569,753	7,329	49.4
Loan.status	Banking	8	570,588	682	11.1
Card.type		8	2,242,680	892	11.8
Gene.fct_growth	Genetics	10	66,855	861	31.9
Gene.loc_nucleus		10	66,855	861	42.5

the number of rows and the number of columns, summed over all tables in the data set. Last not least, the number of learning examples and the distribution of the class attributes are given.

Thus, there are both representatives of classical ILP problems (Trains, KRK, Mutagenesis) as well other problems, mainly from business domains. The sizes of the datasets reach challenging dimensions especially for the latter group of data sets.

Information about software that was used for the experiments can be found in Appendix A.

4.5.3   Procedure

We ensure comparability of the application of several learning systems and of their results by a number of measures.

1. We executed all experiments on the same machine such that the same conditions e. g. of main memory, processor speed, and operating system specifics applied. More specifically, we used a workstation of type Sun-Blade-1000 with 1 GB main memory and an UltraSparc-III processor with 750 MHz. For aspects of the software used, e. g. the version of the operating system, cf. Appendix A.

2. The same point of departure was used for all experiments, viz. our preparations of the data as MySQL databases. In a number of cases, this meant for all learners the usage of a reduced variant of the original data where aspects without relevance for the learning examples or learning task were

left out. This was especially important for ILP systems that were not able to directly use MySQL but had to load all given data into main memory. For more information about the reductions, cf. Appendix B.

3. The input formats for the single learners were produced following conventions for the systems as stated in their documentation or used in earlier research, preferably by the authors of the systems themselves. Still, we took great care to use largely equivalent representations of the data across learning systems. This also applies to the definitions of declarative bias.

4. We applied all learning systems in their respective default schemes. That means that default settings of the parameters were used, if their application was reasonable. This also concerns the declarative biases used.

5. We also tried other preparations of the data and other settings for learning in order to gain a more complete picture of the opportunities of the learning systems.

In summary, we started for all experiments from MySQL (reduced) databases. If necessary, the data were exported into the corresponding formats as input for the learning systems. Bias definitions were also derived from the databases. These steps were supported by tools that we developed for those purposes, cf. Appendix A.

After that, systems were applied in conventional ways with their default settings. For RELAGGS, we were able to use the same implementation that is also used in the following chapter. For the applicability of this implementation, we had to make the exploitation of foreign links and functional dependencies explicit by precomputing a number of joins of the original or reduced tables. Details are given in Appendix B. The times taken for these transformations are recorded in the experimental results section.

We used a setting *branching factor* = 0 for computing these joins. Furthermore, we set *maximum cardinality* = 100 for nominal attributes to be considered for propositionalization. An exception was made for ECML-1998 data, where we used *maximum cardinality* = 10. This exception was made mainly because MySQL tables have a restricted breadth which would have been exceeded otherwise.

The aggregate functions we applied were the following: average, maximum, minimum, and sum for numeric attributes, count of possible values for nominal attributes, and count of related records. In order to unify experiments we did not use the MySQL functions but implementations within RELAGGS. These also had to be used in other experiments with non-standard aggregate functions that are not offered by MySQL.

In the following, we present more information about special settings of the learning systems in our experiments. PROGOL and RSD were also used with non-default parameter settings and on other preparations of the data. These experiments are reported separately.

For TILDE, advanced features of the system such as the opportunity for sampling or chunking were not used, and not either discretization or $\geq$ tests for numeric variables. The latter was remedied for extra experiments that are reported separately. Furthermore, we consistently used test accuracy after pruning as provided in cross-validation result files by TILDE, although there was a second accuracy given there, called "after safe pruning", which was occasionally different.

ROLLUP was simulated with RELAGGS, parameterized in the same way as RELAGGS in the unified experiments, and with joins directly computed with the help of MySQL. Because of main memory limits that made the handling of many Java double variables a high effort for Household.class prediction, we split the target table in four parts for propositionalization, in order to combine the results before propositional learning took place.

After propositionalization by DINUS, RSD, ROLLUP, or RELAGGS, we applied WEKA learners, especially J48 and SMO, both with default parameterizations again.

In order to uniformly arrive at interpretable results, we used stratified 10-fold cross-validation for all experiments. To this end, we developed tools for partitioning the different kinds of input files for the learning systems in a way such that the same partitions included the same sets of examples across learning systems.

Using our own partitionings of the data enabled us to do paired t-tests. Furthermore, advantages with respect to memory usage could be noticed for larger datasets, where e. g. WEKA had difficulties to execute its default cross-validation.

We did not execute multiple cross-validations, although our tools allow for it by the opportunity for the user to specify a seed for the randomizer used during partitioning. Beside the time effort this would have meant e. g. for 10 times 10-fold cross-validation, we rely here on the standard deviations as a means of information. Especially for larger data sets, these are small enough to indicate stability of the results.

We measured classification accuracy or equivalently error, including significances of differences between learning systems, running times, complexities of models and further properties of features across the experimental conditions. For the determination of accuracies or equivalently error rates, we performed stratified 10-fold cross-validation, as stated above.

For running times and complexities of models, we measured training using all available labeled examples. This is an interesting case, because in practice, those models will usually be applied as predictors, based on the assumption that cross-validation results carry over to those models and that learning from more examples leads to higher quality models in general.

Table 4.3: Error rate averages and standard deviations (in percent; n. a. as not applicable for reasons of (1) database schema or (2) running time; best results in **bold**, second best in *italics*)

Target	FOIL	PROGOL	TILDE	DINUS	RSD	RELAGGS
Trains.bound	40.0	30.0	*30.0*	n. a. (1)	40.0	**10.0**
	± 39.4	± 35.0	± 25.8		± 31.6	± 31.6
KRK.illegal	**2.8**	n. a. (2)	24.9	n. a. (1)	*23.8*	27.7
	± 1.1		± 1.2		± 1.5	± 1.1
Muta042.active	22.7	23.3	21.3	18.8	*16.3*	**14.3**
	± 21.7	± 14.0	± 17.4	± 14.3	± 15.3	± 16.0
Muta188.active	**10.2**	18.4	22.3	20.6	22.3	*13.2*
	± 4.9	± 11.1	± 8.2	± 11.6	± 8.2	± 9.1
Partner.class	n. a. (2)	n. a. (2)	n. a. (2)	*19.1*	n. a. (2)	**2.5**
				± 0.2		± 0.5
Household.class	n. a. (2)	n. a. (2)	n. a. (2)	*42.9*	n. a. (2)	**7.1**
				± 2.0		± 0.8
Loan.status	12.7	n. a. (2)	n. a. (2)	*11.1*	n. a. (2)	**7.2**
	± 3.2			± 0.6		± 3.4
Card.type	14.6	n. a. (2)	n. a. (2)	**11.8**	n. a. (2)	*11.8*
	± 2.8			± 0.5		± 2.4
Gene.growth	**10.6**	21.0	19.3	31.9	19.6	*17.9*
	± 2.7	± 3.3	± 3.4	± 0.3	± 4.2	± 4.0
Gene.nucleus	12.8	19.4	**11.6**	37.8	*12.6*	15.0
	± 3.0	± 4.7	± 2.2	± 5.0	± 2.6	± 2.5

Note that we do not include times for loading data into main memory as usual for ILP learners or for producing their input formats in the first place. These times are roughly constant across the experimental conditions and in lower orders of magnitudes than the running times of the learners themselves.

4.5.4 Results

In this section, we first present the results obtained in our unified experiments. Then, we also report results of a series of additional experiments, especially with the learners that serve as points of comparison for RELAGGS, in order to complete the picture. In the final part of this section, we compare our learner to ROLLUP.

Table 4.3 shows, for each of the experimental conditions, the average error across the partitions and the standard deviation. The best results — lowest error, considering deviation in case of a draw — are marked in **bold**.

Table 4.4: Win-loss-tie statistics (row vs. column)

	RSD	DINUS	TILDE	PROGOL	FOIL
RELAGGS	3–2–1	6–0–2	1–2–3	3–0–2	2–2–4
RSD		2–0–2	0–1–5	1–0–4	0–3–3
DINUS			0–2–2	0–2–2	1–3–2
TILDE				2–0–3	0–3–3
PROGOL					0–3–2

Table 4.5: Numbers of columns in results of propositionalization

Target	DINUS	RSD	RELAGGS
Trains20.bound	n. a.	247	57
KRK.illegal	n. a.	321	13
Mutagenesis042.active	5	154	483
Mutagenesis188.active	5	601	483
Partner.class	50	≫100,000	1,078
Household.class	43	≫100,000	1,197
Loan.status	22	≫100,000	1,021
Card.type	22	≫100,000	421
Gene.fct_growth	3	1,052	200
Gene.loc_nucleus	3	1,062	208

Note the partly large standard deviations, especially in cases with relatively few learning examples, as for Trains.bound and Mutagenesis042.active. This makes further considerations as a basis for judgements necessary: statistical significances should be observed. Win-loss-tie statistics are provided in Table 4.4. Decisions about a win or loss are taken here on observing a significance of the differences according to a paired t-test at level $\alpha = 0.05$. Cases in which at least one learner of a pair of learners to be compared was not able to arrive at any model within a day are not counted in this table.

All learning results reported here are based on the usage of J48 after propositionalization, i. e. for DINUS, RSD, and RELAGGS. For the latter, we also used SMO but it turned out to be worse in most cases. There was only one case in which SMO provided significantly better results than J48, viz. for Gene.nucleus with an error rate of 12.4 % ± 2.0 %.

In Table 4.5, column numbers resulting from propositionalization are listed. Those numbers exclude the key attribute, but include the target attribute, i. e. they correspond to the number of attributes as used by WEKA.

Table 4.6: Information gain for best-ranked features (best results in **bold**)

Target	DINUS	RSD	RELAGGS
Trains20.bound	n. a.	**0.493**	**0.493**
KRK.illegal	n. a.	0.005	**0.024**
Mutagenesis042.active	0.342	0.283	**0.474**
Mutagenesis188.active	0.303	0.262	**0.384**
Partner.class	0.081	n. a.	**0.293**
Household.class	0.208	n. a.	**0.570**
Loan.status	0.091	n. a.	**0.136**
Card.type	0.077	n. a.	**0.080**
Gene.fct_growth	0.010	**0.151**	**0.151**
Gene.loc_nucleus	0.030	**0.148**	**0.148**

In Table 4.6, the information gain (IG) is provided for the feature of each appropriate experimental condition that was ranked first by WEKA's corresponding attribute selector.

In Table 4.7, tree sizes for trees as learned from all training data are given as the absolute numbers of nodes they consist of.

In Table 4.8, numbers of clauses as learned from all training data are given, plus numbers of uncovered examples for FOIL and PROGOL. For TILDE, the Prolog notation of trees is used. Those trees cover all examples.

Table 4.9 shows running times for RELAGGS, together with its preparatory and propositional learning phases. Preparation means here the computation of joins, especially exploiting functional dependencies, starting from the same variants of databases as the other systems. Note that we do not look at times for loading data, for instance for WEKA open file. The same applies to reports on running times for other systems such as PROGOL later on. In general, these times are in lower orders of magnitude than those for the actual learning.

Table 4.10 shows the running times for learning from the whole set of training data. For most systems, the times for a single run during cross-validation was in the same order of magnitude than times given in the table. Only for FOIL and one domain, we observed running times that varied strongly: on Gene.growth 3,732.2 sec ± 4,578.3 sec and on Gene.nucleus: 2,568.0 sec ± 4,171.6 sec.

In the following, we report special results achieved with the systems under consideration.

FOIL. For FOIL, we observed partly large differences between learning results depending on the definition which class label would represent the positive class. We provide the best results seen, achieved in most cases by taking the minority class as positive.

Table 4.7: Tree sizes (number of nodes / number of leaves)

Target	DINUS	RSD	RELAGGS
Trains20.bound	n. a.	5 / 3	5 / 3
KRK.illegal	n. a.	2,821 / 1,411	957 / 479
Mutagenesis042.active	5 / 3	5 / 3	9 / 5
Mutagenesis188.active	15 / 8	25 / 13	25 / 13
Partner.class	18 / 13	n. a.	167 / 85
Household.class	4,725 / 4,538	n. a.	290 / 175
Loan.status	1 / 1	n. a.	31 / 16
Card.type	1 / 1	n. a.	21 / 11
Gene.fct_growth	1 / 1	77 / 39	67 / 35
Gene.loc_nucleus	4 / 3	51 / 26	57 / 30

Table 4.8: Numbers of clauses (in parantheses: numbers of uncovered examples)

Target	FOIL	PROGOL	TILDE
Trains20.bound	1 (2)	1 (3)	5 (0)
KRK.illegal	63 (431)	n. a.	1538 (0)
Mutagenesis042.active	3 (1)	3 (4)	3 (0)
Mutagenesis188.active	8 (4)	14 (11)	13 (0)
Partner.class	n. a.	n. a.	n. a.
Household.class	n. a.	n. a.	n. a.
Loan.status	11 (16)	n. a.	n. a.
Card.type	5 (58)	n. a.	n. a.
Gene.fct_growth	14 (41)	32 (106)	49 (0)
Gene.loc_nucleus	10 (54)	97 (39)	36 (0)

Table 4.9: Running times for RELAGGS steps (in seconds)

Target	Preparation	Propositionalization	WEKA-J48
Trains20.bound	0	2	0
KRK.illegal	n. a.	36	36
Mutagenesis042.active	n. a.	8	1
Mutagenesis188.active	n. a.	8	1
Partner.class	52	3,577	1,799
Household.class	35	2,198	427
Loan.status	4	190	12
Card.type	14	445	5
Gene.fct_growth	n. a.	13	6
Gene.loc_nucleus	n. a.	14	6

Table 4.10: Running times (in seconds; for training runs on all examples, best results in **bold**, * — large differences to running times for several partitions during cross-validation)

Target	FOIL	PROGOL	TILDE	DINUS	RSD	RELAGGS
Trains20.bound	3	3	< 1	n. a.	1	2
KRK.illegal	78,946	> 1 d	3,498	n. a.	4,446	72
Muta042.active	1	5	5	< 1	< 1	9
Muta188.active	3	23	82	< 1	3	9
Partner.class	> 1 d	> 1 d	> 1 d	25	> 1 d	5,428
Household.class	> 1 d	> 1 d	> 1 d	6	> 1 d	2,660
Loan.status	3,307	> 1 d	> 1 d	< 1	> 1 d	206
Card.type	1,269	> 1 d	> 1 d	< 1	> 1 d	464
Gene.fct_growth	9,385 *	508	1,239	< 1	48	19
Gene.loc_nucleus	153 *	369	818	< 1	36	20

PROGOL.   Here, we tried the system on the original KRK.illegal problem representation to find out that PROGOL provides good rules after about 17 hours.

TILDE.   This system is not influenced by switching the definition of positive and negative classes, as was the case for FOIL and PROGOL. With the bias chosen for our unified experiments, which was most similar to that of PROGOL and RSD, we did not use many of the potentials of TILDE.

For this reason, we tried some other bias variants. For KRK.illegal, we achieved with another bias allowing for "old" variables in more argument positions a number of 808 Prolog rules after 5,473 sec. The first of those rules corresponds to a specific case of adjacency, which was an explicit predicate in the original problem representation. We saw an error in stratified ten-fold cross-validation of 9.3%±0.7%.

For Partner.class and Household.class, we could not achieve any results, not even after manually dropping nominal attributes with more than 10 distinct values, while for Loan.status, we at least saw a first rule after about 3 hours, which asked for a criterion known to be highly relevant in the domain.

With greater-than tests for numeric attributes, TILDE achieved after 82 sec with a model of 13 Prolog rules an error rate of 14.3±8.0 for Mutagenesis188.active, which is significantly better than above, and makes significant differences to FOIL and RELAGGS disappear. For Loan.status prediction, missing values caused the system to fault. We only arrived at any results after excluding table *trans*, which made a good solution impossible here. For other problems, we observed no significant changes.

RSD.   We also tried RSD on original representations of some of the problems and reached some notable results. For KRK.illegal, using a special parameter setting in order to avoid an explosion of the number of features, we even produced an error rate of 0 % with a tree consisting of 153 nodes based on 84 features after about 4,400 sec. For Mutagenesis188.active, we achieved 12.2 % error with a tree consisting of 11 nodes and based on 26 features after about 15 min.

Back on problem representations as used for our unified experiments, we tried measures such as manually dropping numeric attributes. This helped only for Loan.status prediction, where the system reached an error of 7.2 % with a tree consisting of 23 nodes based on 3,058 features after about 1,330 sec. For Household.class, restricted to nominal attributes with at most 10 different values, we allowed the system to run for longer than a day, and after about 4.5 days, including WEKA learning with J48 taking about 11,500 sec for the complete training set, a tree was produced from 3,499 features that had an error of 32.1%±1,8% in stratified 10-fold cross-validation.

We now turn to results achieved with ROLLUP.

Table 4.11: ROLLUP vs. RELAGGS: Experimental results for selected learning tasks

Target	Approach:	ROLLUP	RELAGGS
Partner.class	Error rate average:	5.2 %	2.5 %
	Error rate std. dev.:	± 0.9 %	± 0.5 %
	Number of features:	519	1,078
	IG of best feature:	0.25	0.29
	Size of tree	303 / 161	167 / 85
	Running time:	3,377 sec	5,428 sec
Household.class	Error rate average:	7.5 %	7.1 %
	Error rate std. dev.:	± 0.8 %	± 0.8 %
	Number of features:	1,896	1,197
	IG of best feature:	0.57	0.57
	Size of tree	435 / 345	290 / 175
	Running time:	5,531 sec	2,660 sec

ROLLUP. Table 4.11 shows results for ROLLUP on two learning tasks, in comparison to RELAGGS. For the other learning tasks, results of the two systems are the same. This is due to the absence of multiple one-to-many relationships on paths induced by the other database schemas. Even if there are these circumstances to be met, as is the case for Trains.bound and Loan.status, the actual data do occasionally obey to a simpler one-to-one relationship, as between cars and loads, and between loans and accounts.

The difference in accuracy for Partner.class prediction is highly significant, while it is insignificant for Household.class prediction, according to a t-test in the same variant as used above.

4.5.5   Discussion

Error rate averages

The results concerning errors of the learning systems used in our experiments as reported in Table 4.3 offer a number of surprising and remarkable aspects.

The first unexpected circumstance is that RELAGGS seems to be the overall winner here with delivering the best result in 5 cases and the second best in another 3 cases. In past experiments, we had seen a superiority of RELAGGS on Loan.status, Partner.class, and Household.class prediction compared to variants of DINUS and PROGOL [71], and also good performance on Trains.bound, Gene.growth, and Gene.nucleus prediction compared to RSD [65].

However, our experiments here included more learning systems, especially FOIL and TILDE, and more learning tasks, especially a new variant of KRK.illegal and — last not least — Card.type prediction. Thus, we did not expect such a clear result in favor of RELAGGS.

The second unexpected point is the good appearance of FOIL, actually presenting the follow-up for RELAGGS with the winning result in 3 cases. Initially, we thought that TILDE would have better opportunities to reach such results. In fact, of the many opportunities of TILDE, we restricted ourselves to those comparable with the other learners here. Still, our settings are a plausible way to use TILDE, and to arrive at better settings produces a certain additional search effort.

We further judge it remarkable that PROGOL did not arrive at any results in the amount of time allowed in half of the cases. This is not completely unexpected, though, since complexity issues are known to be problematic for PROGOL. Further, the kind of learning tasks largely deviates from those that PROGOL typically excels at, viz. those with less data points but more complex structures as in a number of natural language learning problems.

It may also be remarkable that RELAGGS did *not* win on Gene.growth here, despite of the success in the KDD Cup 2001. So it could well have been the case that an application of FOIL would have beaten our solution. However, there seems no solution to have been produced yet which is better than our overall solution, as reported by Atramentov and colleagues in 2003 [5]. This may have to do with the more complex overall task, where n of m functions had to be predicted.

Looking at the learning task of KRK.illegal prediction, the good result achieved by FOIL indicates that our preparation of the data was not only plausible but also appropriate for learning in principle.

Statistical significances

The evaluation of error rates was done so far mainly with respect to their average values. Of course, this is not conclusive in itself. We have also to consider other statistical descriptors. Here, we first note partly high standard deviations of the error rates accross cross-validation folds. This is why we provide statistical significance results in Table 4.4. This helps to evaluate the results seen so far in more detail.

As we see from the comparison of RELAGGS to RSD, TILDE, and FOIL in the first line of the body of that table, there can be no overall preference for RELAGGS. In six comparisons, it is significantly better than the competitors, but in another six comparisons, it is significantly worse.

Still, we see RELAGGS as an interesting option to test when high accuracies are in the primary focus of learning. Moreover, if we would have considered each case, where another learner did not arrive at any results in a reasonable amount of time, as predicting the majority class, the results with respect to statistical significance would have looked much more favorable for RELAGGS.

The last column in the win-loss-tie table confirms the strength of FOIL on the learning tasks of our experiments. Also, the weakness of PROGOL is confirmed, also that of the variant of DINUS, which was expected for this rather simple approach, while TILDE looks better here, with more significant wins than losses compared to RELAGGS and wins/ties only compared to RSD, DINUS, and PROGOL.

Overall, the error rate results show that our learner RELAGGS is competitive w. r. t. both prominent ILP learners and typical traditional approaches to propositionalization. Thus, the system seems to be sufficient in a number of cases. In some other cases, however, ILP approaches seem to have the more appropriate means for high quality models. The latter indicates a confirmation of WH1A, i. e. superiority of ILP approaches. Our working hypothesis can be extended, however, to also state that RELAGGS is in fact sufficient to reach low error rates in many cases.

WH2A can not be completely confirmed in the light of the comparison of RE-LAGGS and RSD. Traditional approaches to propositionalization as represented by RSD can obviously produce better models in a number of cases. However, it is true that difficulties with numeric data limit their applicability, in favor of RELAGGS.

Feature sets

An important factor for the approaches to propositionalization are the feature sets produced, especially the numbers of features and an indicator of their quality. Table 4.5 shows the numbers of features produced by DINUS, RSD, and RELAGGS that serve as input for propositional learners. As expected, DINUS produces comparatively low numbers of features, because it makes only restricted use of the tables in the databases.

A more interesting comparison is possible for the latter two systems. In most cases, RSD produces more features here than RELAGGS, occasionally even a number considered too high for further consideration, viz. >100,000. This is due to the lack of an appropriate handling for numeric attributes. Leaving them out was in some cases able to change the number of features down to the same order of magnitude as that of RELAGGS.

However, the error rates remained relatively high, which is probably due to leaving out numeric attributes. Also, efficiency was still not convincing. In general, it is interesting to note that RSD produces higher numbers of features than RELAGGS although RSD uses class information in the process of feature construction: RSD produces more complex features than RELAGGS that ask for the occurrence of certain combinations of values for different attributes.

This complexity seems not sufficient here for the construction of high-quality features, though. Instead, RELAGGS shows consistently the best attributes in its results according to the information gain criterion. First of all, this seems to be a confirmation that aggregation as applied by RELAGGS is a good idea. Further, better features raise hopes for better models. Of course, looking at the best feature only can at best be a rough indicator for other features in the sets. Still, we think it is an illustrative point.

Model complexities

We now turn to model complexity and thus our WH1B/WH2B. For the propositionalization systems as reported in Table 4.7, DINUS delivers the smallest trees, with the exception of Household.class prediction, where a giant but flat tree is produced because of the lack of simple and strongly predictive features.

The tree sizes for RSD and RELAGGS are in the same order of magnitude. Further, with node numbers below 100, trees have a chance to be comprehensible for human experts in a majority of cases here.

For the ILP systems as documented in Table 4.8, the situation is similar. In most cases, rule set sizes are in the same order of magnitude across systems per learning task.

A notable exception is the comparatively small rule set created by FOIL for KRK.illegal prediction, which signals also the model's quality w. r. t. accuracy. Further, the uncovered examples can be regarded as treated by another clause or rule that predicts their majority class. Precise figures are provided just for a more detailed impression of the models.

Trees resulting from propositional learning can be translated into a number of rules corresponding to the number of their leaves. Based on such translations, we gain the following picture.

While the numbers of rules are in most cases in the same order of magnitude, FOIL produces often models distinctly smaller than those by PROGOL, TILDE, RSD, and RELAGGS, with less than half of their sizes. Having also in mind the strong results of FOIL w. r. t. model accuracy, this enforces the suspicion that FOIL's mechanisms to create good rules and to control model complexity are effective here.

Those observations for FOIL seem to confirm our WH1B, while results for PROGOL and TILDE show that the assumption is not true in general. Also, we must differentiate for WH2B: DINUS shows the expected small models but RELAGGS is not distinctly superior to RSD w. r. t. model complexity.

Efficiency

We find our WH1C/WH2C fully confirmed by the experimental data. With a growing data set size and complexity, RELAGGS is the only well-scaling approach beside the restricted variant of DINUS, as expected. During experiments, we observed that main memory limitations were not responsible for the longer running times of the other systems.

Instead, search in large hypothesis spaces caused high costs here, while RE-LAGGS avoids such search processes altogether. Thus, the bias of RELAGGS is useful and — in the light of results for model accuracy and complexity — suggests a preference for the application of our approach or well-designed aggregation approaches in general.

ROLLUP vs. RELAGGS

For most of our learning tasks, results of ROLLUP and RELAGGS are equivalent. Effects occur only for databases with deeper structure, i. e. longer paths in the induced graphs from the target relation node to other nodes. This is exemplified with the Partner.class and Household.class data.

For Partner.class, the farthest node `tfkomp` can be reached from the target relation node `part` by exploiting 3 foreign key relationships including 2 one-to-many relationships, cf. Figure B.5 in Appendix B. It takes 4 such steps including 3 one-to-many relationships from `hhold` to `tfkomp` for Household.class prediction. This difference is responsible for the change from less time consumption by ROLLUP for Partner.class prediction to more time consumption for Household.class prediction, compared to RELAGGS. This indicates a confirmation for WH3A.

WH3B is also confirmed by our results: ROLLUP does not produce better models here than RELAGGS. There is even a statistically significant difference in performance to be observed for Partner.class prediction in favor of RELAGGS.

Trees vs. SVMs

We have to reject our final WH4 concerning expectations w. r. t. support-vector machine learning. Most results of the application of WEKA's SMO to outputs of RELAGGS were not better than those reached with J48. Only in one case, a statistically significantly better result was produced. Even that was not an overall winning solution. Thus, we can not confirm that the application of SMO was a valueable venture in our experiments, although support-vector machine learners are supposed to be able to deal well with large numbers of moderately relevant features.

Furthermore, the application of J48 can be recommended because of the interpretability of the results, which may be essential especially in cases of semantics-blind feature construction as performed by RELAGGS. Nevertheless, experiments reported in the following chapter show that the application of SMO can be fruitful under certain conditions in the context of propositionalization as well.

Ease of use

Finally, we discuss aspects of ease of use. Clearly, this topic is more diffult to judge than effectivity and efficiency of learning, since it depends on the user.

However, a general impression that we gained during our experiments was that there are two circumstances favorable for RELAGGS.

First, working directly with DBMS makes the construction of mode declaration files unnecessary. The production of those files can cause a high effort for the user.

Second, we use comparatively few parameters for propositionalization. Here, there were in fact only two of them: for setting the branching factor and the maximum allowed cardinality of nominal attributes. Effects especially of the latter parameter setting are also easy to understand.

4.5.6   Further Related Work

Blockeel and Bruynooghe [13] observed that relational learners handle (multi-) sets of values either by aggregation or by selecting specific elements, the latter of which is comparable to existence checks. Although this was not completely true — for instance, even the basic variant of RELAGGS as used in this chapter includes counting of possible values for nominal attributes, which means effectively to first select, then aggregate — the authors make a number of interesting proposals for a combination of aggregation and selection. Especially, they introduce the idea to apply recurrent neural networks for *learning* aggregate functions.

Knobbe and colleagues [55] took their approach to the application of aggregate functions further by including them into the construction of the final hypothesis. The authors describe relevant aspects of aggregate functions for this purpose, e. g. monotonicity, where e. g. minimima can only get smaller when new values are added to the summarized (multi-)set. However, this kind of dynamic aggregation seems to involve search problems that may affect efficiency.

Jensen and Neville [48] describe an interesting phenomenon in the context of aggregation: degree disparity. This notion means that the number of objects related to target objects may correlate with class labels. This affects certain results of aggregate functions. The authors provide the example of movies, which may be the more successful the more actors participate. Then, aggregate function results such as sums of the actors' ages will show some correlation with class labels as well, although age as such may have nothing to do with a movie's success.

The authors [48] observe overcomplex models resulting from the occurrence of degree disparity, beside possible irritations of analysts. In our experiments, we did not control for degree disparity, such that models may be too complex. However, our model evaluation included checks of the features in the rules and trees, at least of those near the roots, which did not hint at problems here.

4.6 Summary

In this section, we explained our choice of clause sets $\mathcal{C}$ on which proposition-alization should be based. Ideas of foreign links and of functional dependencies ensured that such sets $\mathcal{C}$ remained comparatively small and thus efficiently to handle.

We introduced the application of aggregate functions for propositionalization and provided an algorithm for propositionalization in this spirit. We illustrated the workings of the algorithm with a number of examples drawing on our running example.

For closely related work, we then discussed common aspects and differences in detail. We believe that the different approaches can promote each other in the future and be combined in favorable ways.

Finally, we presented an exhaustive empirical investigation, which compares prominent ILP learners and several approaches to propositionalization including different propositional learners. The results of our experiments show that our approach to propositionalization reached a good point in the spectrum of effec-tivity vs. efficiency. RELAGGS turned out to be competitive with other current approaches to relational learning.

Chapter 5

Exploiting Database Technology

In the preceding chapter, we already began to exploit ideas that are common in the database area, first of all with the application of the standard aggregate functions that can be found included in DBMS. Moreover, their usage in a data-type specific way was supported by information contained in database schemas. Schema information was also relevant for foreign links and functional dependencies.

In this chapter, we take the approach even further. The first central issue here is based on the observation of computation costs of the algorithm as applied so far. Here, a crucial factor is the same as noted often before, also in the context of ILP [133, 135]: the computation of joins of several relations. We suggest a method to replace expensive joins by comparatively cheap ones, which results in considerable efficiency gains. This concerns the whole process of learning, not only in the context of propositionalization, but also for other approaches to multi-relational learning.

The second important point is the extension of the spectrum of aggregate functions to be applied. Here, the consideration of types becomes more differentiated, influenced by typical atomic types as found in relational databases. So far, we distinguished *numeric* and *nominal* attributes, as usual in KDD. Now, we further distinguish *numeric* into *integer* and *real-valued* with different sets of aggregate functions to be applied. This indicates only a range of opportunities for further enhancements, e. g. including special aggregate functions for *date* and *time* attributes.

A third topic is related to the usage of key attributes. For RDB, the concept of keys is of highest relevance. In conventional KDD with a one-table input, identifiers are often neglected. Of course, if identifiers do not contain any information except that necessary for keeping objects apart, they do not have any predictive value. However, key attributes often carry more information, even in the conventional case. In the multi-relational scenario, there can be even more situations when it seems advisable not to completely ignore identifying values for learning.

Fourth, we consider aspects of results of propositionalization such as the extent and further handling of redundant and otherwise irrelevant features. This is not directly related to database-specific issues, however, extends the basic variant of our approach as introduced in the preceding chapter.

A thourough empirical investigation into the issues mentioned above and further elaborated in the following sections is a further main part of this chapter.

5.1 Pre-Processing for Propositionalization

5.1.1 Idea of New Star Schemas

Join costs are a major component in multi-relational learning. Consider a target table that has one-to-many relationships to n other tables, each with m rows. Then, the computation of a natural join has complexity of m^n, if for each record in the target table, each record in the second table has to be checked, then each record in the third table, and so forth. For RELAGGS, this case can be excluded by setting the branching factor to zero.

However, the situation is the same for a join of several tables, starting from the target relation, with a chain of n one-to-many relationships from one table to the other. Here, RELAGGS in its basic variant as introduced in the preceding chapter would be inefficient.

Furthermore, there are usually different paths in the relational database graph from the target relation to other relations, which takes the number of possible joins to infinity — even with the restriction to natural joins as used here. And beside join computation complexity, the resulting relations can become large as well, w. r. t. not only row numbers but also column numbers, as roughly the sums of column numbers of all relations involved.

Our analysis of the ROLLUP algorithm by Knobbe and colleagues [54], cf. Chapter 4, showed that those aspects of complexity were dealt with there in a favorable way. By recursively aggregating and joining tables at the current distance d_{cur} from the target relation to related tables at distance $d_{cur} - 1$, some complex joins are avoided.

This inspired us to have the following idea. Instead of getting distant tables successively closer to the target relation by the ROLLUP mechanisms, we bring information from the target relation to the distant tables such that they can be aggregated in their near-original form and then cheaply joined directly to the target table.

The information to be conveyed for this purpose are obviously the target identifiers, such that they can serve as criteria for grouping rows of other tables before aggregation. Thus, we proposed to propagate target object identifiers to the other relations such that finally all other relations have a foreign key attribute pointing to the primary key attribute of the target relation [74]. We applied this

idea successfully in several learning situations before [67]. We present more details
about new star generation and properties in the following.

Note that the schema resulting from target identifier propagation is different
from the well-known *star schema* in typical data warehouses [6], where it is the
central facts table that contains foreign key attributes pointing to the primary
key attributes of the surrounding dimension tables. Still, the overall star shape
of the schema is predominant, so we chose to give ours the working title "new
star" schema. Figure 5.1 presents the running example database in such a new
star schema.

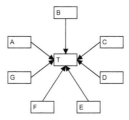

Figure 5.1: The running example database in a new star schema (arrows represent
foreign key relationships)

Note that ROLLUP, with the obvious setting of $d = 1$, and RELAGGS, with a
setting of the branching factor to zero, behave largely in the same way when the
input is in the form of such a new star schema.

5.1.2   An Algorithm for Schema Transformation

In the following, we describe a way to derive new star schema databases from
original relational databases. It ultimately relies on a combination of automatic
measures with human decisions and control.

We expect as input a relational database with single-attribute primary keys
for all tables. This corresponds to recommendations for efficient database design,
often taken further to the suggestion to use integer key attributes. If this situation
is not given, it can be achieved by enumerating objects represented in tables, if
each object is represented by exactly one row there. If not, normalization steps
could help.

We further expect primary key attributes in the original database to be indexed for efficient retrieval of selected rows of tables. This again is usual in
database design. We do *not* expect foreign key attributes to be indexed, as might
not be the case for relational databases because of the management cost for indexes.

Basically, we now intend to generate a new database with a new star schema with read-only access to the original database. We assume this intention to be in line with practical demands for KDD processes not to increase work loads on databases that are first of all in use for other purposes.

For the expected situation, it is implicit that we have only two basic types of relationships between tables: one-to-many and many-to-one. Many-to-many relationships are modeled with the help of two appropriate relationships of those other two types. Further, one may further elaborate on zero-or-one-to-zero-or-more relationships. We abstain from doing that here and only hint at the opportunities of dealing with these issues with the help of appropiate outer joins.

Then, starting from a copy of the target table in the new database with its primary key attribute kept, the relationships of the original target table to the surrounding tables in the original database are checked. For each relationship, if it is one-to-many, the non-target table contains target identifiers already in a corresponding foreign key attribute. Thus, a simple copy can be made for the new database. If it is a many-to-one relationship, an additional foreign key attribute can be produced and filled appropriately for a derived table in the new database.

The situation is more complex when we get further away from the target relation. The first of two tables considered in each propagation step can be assumed to be situated in the new database and already equipped with a target identifier attribute.

Further, before propagation, the first and the second table in the original database must have been in either (a) a one-to-many or (b) many-to-one relationship. Exploiting these relationships, the target identifiers can now be further propagated. For (a), an index should be created for the former primary key attribute of the first table in the new database that can speed up the join. For (b), there is the primary key index in the second table in the original database that can serve the same purpose. Table 5.1 provides an algorithm for target identifier propagation.

Example 35 *For our running example, the first steps according to the algorithm would work in the following way.*

Copies of all relations in the original database form R_1. The target relation t *is moved from R_1 to M_1. Since it is the only relation in M_1, it is chosen for further expansion of the new database. Directly related tables are* a, d, f, *and* g. *These relations are stored in M_2. For* a, *target identifiers need not be propagated, because there is a corresponding foreign key attribute already, similar for* d. *For* f, *target identifier propagation can be achieved with a MySQL statement such as the following, assuming the original data are hold in a database* test_we, *and the current database is a new one:*

```
create table f (key (t_id), key (f_id))
select t.t_id, f.*
```

Table 5.1: Identifier propagation algorithm

---

1. **Accept** as input: a set of relations R_1 (copy of the original database) with schema information (keys, types, ...), with one of the relations marked as target; initially empty sets M_1, M_2, and R_2

2. **Move** target relation from R_1 to M_1

3. **While** M_1 is not empty do

    (a) **Choose** a relation $r \in M_1$

    (b) **Determine** all relations $\{q \mid q \in R_1\}$ reachable from r using a foreign key relationship and move those relations from R_1 to M_2

    (c) **While** M_2 is not empty do

        i. **Choose** a relation $q \in M_2$
        ii. **Propagate** target identifiers from r to q (details in the main text)
        iii. **Move** q from M_2 to M_1

    (d) MOVE r from M_1 to R_2

4. **Output** R_2 (database in new star schema)

```
from t, test_we.f
where t.f_id = f.f_id;
```

Identifier propagation works similarly for table g. *After propagation, the four tables are moved from M_2 to M_1, while the target table leaves M_1 for the result database R_2.*

In a second iteration, say, a *is chosen from M_1 first. Then, M_2 is formed by* b *and* c, *which will get the target identifiers from* a *with the help of statements similar to the one shown for* f, *and so forth.*

5.1.3 Treatment of Cyclic Graphs

The identifier propagation algorithm as provided in Table 5.1 works — with the same results independently of the implementation of "choose" procedures — for databases with acyclic undirected graphs induced by the original relational database schema. For the general case, i.e. with circles in that graph, we see human intervention as favorable. Based on considerations of complexity and semantics, the user may decide in favor of one of a series of opportunities here. A collection is enumerated in the following.

1. For instance, the user may decide to only use the resulting table from identifier propagation on (one of) the shortest path(s) from the target relation to the original table.

2. Alternatively, results of identifier propagation on different paths through the relational database graph may be combined by a (multi-)set operator such as for union or the RDB-typical union all.

3. As a further alternative, result tables from using different paths may be kept and used separately in subsequent steps.

In our experiments, we see examples of those different treatments of the original data.

1. For Partner.class prediction, we used only the result of one path to table tfkomp, viz. via vvert, since more would have further increased cost. Moreover, this result was a superset of the tfkomp rows reachable via tfrol.

2. For Loan.status prediction, we united the data describing districts for customers and for bank branches.

3. For Gene.growth prediction, on the other hand, we kept information about the gene in the current focus of learning and about its neighbors apart, assuming a higher relevance of the former and that those data could be hidden in the neighbors' data if united with them.

There are automatic approaches to dealing with circles in the RDB graph as well, e. g. with ROLLUP's depth parameter. However, corresponding to our experience with KDD projects, it is valuable for the analyst to closely observe processes such as those for identifier propagation. It provides an appropriate level of control for the user. Moreover, the user can develop a better understanding for the data and even intuitions about how to best deal with them.

The sketch of the algorithm above corresponds largely to our approach taken for the experiments reported later in this chapter, cf. also Appendix C. However, there may be even more efficient ways for propagation, e. g. using extra tables that consist of the relevant key columns only. Also, class labels could be propagated along with target identifiers to allow for supervised aggregation in the style of RCC based systems [96]. These further approaches were considered to be beyond the scope of this dissertation.

5.1.4   Information Loss and Materialization

An important property of the process of target identifier propagation as presented above is the circumstance that no information is lost here. Since all columns of the original relations are kept and there is at maximum an enrichment with the target identifier column and a possible multiplication of the original rows corresponding to the relationships with target objects, the original relations can be reconstructed completely from a database in the new star schema.

Data may be left out during the process, if data items in non-target tables are in no way related to the target objects. This was done for our experiments, but if reconstruction of the whole original database is of interest, the application of appropriate outer joins to build new stars is the method of choice.

At this point, we discuss advantages and disadvantages of materializing new star databases as suggested above, contrary to opportunities to read the data for propositionalization or for other kinds of multi-relational learning directly from the original databases on demand.

As advantages, we see the following:

- The cost of materializing new stars is about the same as that of selecting the relevant data from the relational database for further processing. However, if multiple runs of propositionalization, say with different parameter settings, should be performed, cost of materialization occurs only once, while that of data extraction from the original database would arise for each run of propositionalization.

- If ordering of rows by target identifiers is included in new star generation, this can be favorably executed during materialization.

- There is no repeated work load put on the original databases, when new star computation results are materialized.

- Archiving new stars as the starting points for further data analyses can be favorable.

- In the course of building new stars, other data preparation tasks can be performed as well, e. g. the choice of minimum sufficient data types, codings for nominal values, projections w. r. t. relevancy of columns, and many more.

A special example of feature construction hand in hand with new star generation can be observed within the preparation for Loan.status prediction. There, table client contained an attribute combining information about gender and birthday of the client. We decided to prefer two separate attributes for these pieces of information. The split is also documented in Appendix C. In that appendix, the reader can also find the restriction of considered transactions to those that occurred before the corresponding loans were granted. Another example was our approach to deal with interaction information in the Gene data [22] that in effect led to a new star schema.

Disadvantages of new star materialization may be posed by the extra effort for managing the new star databases, similarly to the results of propositionalization as mentioned at the beginning of Chapter 3. Also, care has to be taken with changing original databases: dynamic adaptations of new stars and learning results are not yet dealt with in our proposals.

5.1.5 New Star Schemas vs. Universal Relations

In the following, we investigate issues of universal relations that are occasionally suggested as a simple way to deal with problems of multi-relational learning. We do not focus here on the problem that a learning example would usually be represented by several rows in a universal relation. This could be handled exactly by aggregation, again. However, universal relations show a tendency to quickly explode, contrary to new stars, as we illustrate with an example.

Example 36 *Figure 5.2 repeats a part of our running example database schema, for the convenience of the reader. The schema already fulfills demands for new stars, such that no further steps are necessary before applying* RELAGGS.

The natural join of relations T, A, *and* D *is depicted in Figure 5.3. Such joins would be used to produce a UR for our running example database. Even for this small example, there are notable size differences: before the join, there are 58 data values in the database extract. After the join, there are 156 values, because of the introduction of redundancies, even though redundant foreign key attributes were omitted here. In the general case, it can easily be imagined that the size of the join results is explosive with the number of tables related to each other in the same way as it is the case here.*

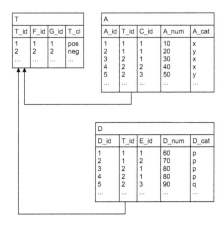

Figure 5.2: Relations T, A, and D from our running example database

There are joins for identifier propagation involved in new star generation in the order of the number of relations in the original database, usually. In each of these joins, there are only two relations concerned, which makes the process rather efficient.

However, the number of rows in relations with propagated identifiers can grow large such that the user should watch the process and take appropriate measures.

Aggregation can then be executed on single tables, which is also possible in an efficient way, especially if rows are ordered by target identifiers. Finally, the aggregated tables have to be joined to the target relation. This means $n-1$ joins with n as the number of relations in the new star schema. Moreover, the target relation is in a one-to-one relationship with each aggregated table from the new star database, such that these joins are cheap, again, especially for ordered data.

5.2 Query Result Processing

5.2.1 Non-Standard Aggregate Functions

Within the term project by Streuer [124] and for the diploma thesis by Körnig [57], RELAGGS was extended by a number of aggregate functions that are non-standard in the sense that they are not provided by SQL as such. The extensions were made hoping for positive effects for learning by the production of further predictive features.

Those non-standard aggregate functions include standard deviations and ranges, i. e. the difference of maximum and minimum values, for numeric attributes.

| T_A_D | | | | | | | | | | | |
T_id	F_id	G_id	T_cl	A_id	C_id	A_num	A_cat	D_id	E_id	D_num	D_cat
1	1	1	pos	1	1	10	x	1	1	60	p
1	1	1	pos	1	1	10	x	2	2	70	p
1	1	1	pos	2	1	20	y	1	1	60	p
1	1	1	pos	2	1	20	y	2	2	70	p
2	2	2	neg	3	1	30	x	3	1	80	p
2	2	2	neg	3	1	30	x	4	1	80	p
2	2	2	neg	3	1	30	x	5	3	90	q
2	2	2	neg	4	2	40	x	3	1	80	p
2	2	2	neg	4	2	40	x	4	1	80	p
2	2	2	neg	4	2	40	x	5	3	90	q
2	2	2	neg	5	3	50	y	3	1	80	p
2	2	2	neg	5	3	50	y	4	1	80	p
2	2	2	neg	5	3	50	y	5	3	90	q
...	...	...	...	...	...	...	...	...	...	...	...

Figure 5.3: Natural join of relations T, A, and D

Standard deviations are actually often offered by DBMS, although not contained in the SQL standard. Range information seemed to be possibly useful, and at least easy to compute.

Further, medians, 1-quartiles and 3-quartiles are computed for integer attributes. They were expected to be more stable against outliers in the data than the usual average used so far. For integer attributes as well as for nominal attributes, the number of different values is counted.

For nominal attributes only, the mode is considered, as well as relative frequencies of possible values and exists tests for possible values. The two latter functions were chosen in order to allow for a comparison with the usage of absolute frequencies of possible values as done before, as a partial result of Körnig's thesis. For more details, the reader is referred to Appendix A.

A further extension was made with the introduction of conditional aggregation. Here, we use an additional restriction before aggregation, viz. on the value of one of the nominal attributes that describe the objects in focus of aggregation. For example, using the Trains.bound data, a feature could now express the average number of wheels of a train's long cars only.

As it turned out, this extension often results in explosive sizes of resulting feature sets. That is why additional parameters were introduced for RELAGGS. First, the number of possible values for the nominal attribute that forms the conditions can be restricted. Second, the number of missing values in the resulting feature can be restricted.

Körnig [57] also introduced a further global parameter to constrain the usage of nominal values. Here, not all possible values are counted as before but only those that occur for a certain percentage of the learning examples. While this seems a good way to avoid the creation of irrelevant or weak features, we did not use this option in our experiments in order to ensure comparability with former results.

Considering the wide range of possible aggregate functions, our choice is motivated by considerations of simple computation and certain relationships to standard aggregate functions, as mentioned at the beginning of this subsection. Domain experts may often be in the position to design further aggregate functions that are promising for the solution of learning tasks at hand. However, one of our intentions here is to investigate the results that can be achieved without possibly expensive experts' advice but based on rather simple aggregate functions only.

5.2.2   Usage of Key Information

In a usual scenario for KDD, identifiers of learning examples are not used for learning. When it comes to learning aspects common to the examples, identifiers can not be of help, being different for the examples by their very nature. Moreover, new test examples will have different identifiers as well, such that models that take decisions based on identifier values of the old training examples may not be applicable in a reasonable way.

Contrary to that usual scenario, values for primary key attributes are in practice often computed in a way such that identifiers do carry additional information beyond their ability to distinguish the represented objects. For instance, by drawing subsequent numbers on demand, i. e. inserts into database tables, to form the primary key values, there is order information about inserts encoded in those identifiers, maybe even information about insertion time and aspects dependent on that. If used with care, such information can be useful for learning and the application of its results.

In a multi-relational learning scenario, there are even further opportunities for useful identifiers, viz. those in tables different from the target relation. Those values may even be the only values present to distinguish between positive and negative examples, as illustrated with the following example.

Example 37 *Figure 5.4 presents an extension of our running example in order to illustrate an effect possible w. r. t. identifiers.*

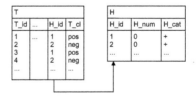

Figure 5.4: An extension to the running example database for the demonstration of an effect w. r. t. identifiers: *H_id* as an attribute with predictive power

Here, table H *shows constant values for its attributes apart from the key attribute. Exactly those key values, however, are perfect predictors for the training examples. If a test example from the same population should be classified, this can be done based on those identifiers, with the same optimism as usual in KDD.*

5.3 Post-Processing

In unsupervised propositionalization, it is plausible to assume that many features are produced which can not contribute to good models to be learned. There may be irrelevant features, e. g. trivial cases of attributes with only one value occurring or the somewhat more complicated case of attributes with no relationship to the target attribute at all. Also, there may be pairwise redundant features, e. g. showing the same values for the same learning examples.

Relevant questions in this context are: What is the extent of those counter-productive features in propositionalization results? What should be done against this phenomenon?

In traditional propositionalization, there were methods developed for irrelevancy treatment that are tailored to Boolean result tables from propositionalization [77]. For RELAGGS, we deal with the more demanding case of result tables from propositionalization that contain numeric and nominal values. We investigated issues about irrelevancy treatment in this situation on several occasions [72, 73]. We experimented with fast detection of redundancy and opportunities to select features accordingly. Best results, however, could be achieved by applying simple filters for feature subset selection. These methods are also part of the empirical studies reported on below.

Here, we drop features before propositional learning, which do not show an information gain above zero considering the whole training data set. Obviously, this is a heuristic approach, since an attribute that shows no information gain for the complete training set may well do so for some subset. We still hope for positive effects not only with respect to efficiency of the whole process but also for effectivity of learning, since smaller hypothesis spaces can be favorable as is well-known in KDD.

Of course, the best way would be to avoid the production of irrelevant features. This could be achieved by two-phase propositionalization: first in a supervised way based on a sample of the training data, including the evaluation of produced features, and following in an unsupervised way to produce only the highly-evaluated features. This approach, however, is not in the scope of this thesis.

Another issue of post-processing is that of specific feature construction for results from propositionalization. Beside conventional feature construction, we might apply some functions here that use knowledge about the origin of the attributes in the propositionalization result, for instance to produce averages from counts and sums only after the main aggregation process, or ranges from maxima and minima.

It remains for further investigations if decisions about when to compute which aggregate function values could lead to higher efficiency. The same applies to functions that would consider not only one original attribute and its descendants but even features originating from different original tables. Here, results of aggregating expensive join results such as the *T-A-D* join in Example 36 could be produced in a way avoiding that join, basically by taking the appropriate counts from one table as multipliers for aggregates of the other table.

Example 38 *Regarding counts for possible values of* A_cat *grouped by* T_id, *we see from the original table* A *for* T_id = 1 *a value of 1 for* x *(1) and a value of 1 for* y *(2), for* T_id = 2 *a value of 2 for* x *(3) and again a value of 1 for* y *(4). For the expensive join of table* T, A, *and* D, *those counts are 2 (1), 2 (2), 6 (3), and 3 (4). So, the proportions between those values across learning examples have changed, which may be a source for interesting learning results. Moreover, the change can be seen as a weighting of* A_cat *by the number of entries in table* D. *The* T-A-D *values can be produced from the* T-A *values by multiplication with the counts of related records in* D.

5.4 Empirical Evaluation

5.4.1 Objectives

We conduct a series of experiments to find out about effects of the usage of databases in a new star schema compared to the original data, mainly for our RELAGGS approach, but also for other learners. Further, we study effects of using more aggregate functions, of considering identifier attributes during propositionalization and of applying simple feature subset selection techniques.

Our working hypotheses are the following.

WH5.1A From using databases in a new star schema, we expect further efficiency gains. RELAGGS, although comparatively well-scaling already, cf. Section 4.5, can even be accelerated in this way.

WH5.1B At the same time, we hope for the information loss not to enlarge error rates significantly. This information loss originates from leaving out joins involving more than two tables. Actually, there might be even positive effects caused by the implicit kind of feature selection and redundancy avoidance.

WH5.1C Model complexity should be lower based on narrower results of propositionalization.

WH5.2A The introduction of more aggregate functions into the process of propositionalization bears potentials for higher quality features. We hope for them to be useful during learning, instead of the attribute space of higher dimensionality to misguide learning.

WH5.2B Compared to the usage of original database schemas, there should be efficiency gains from using new stars, even with enlarged sets of aggregate functions applied to new stars.

WH5.2C Model complexity might even be lowered compared to the usage of purely standard aggregate functions on new star schema databases, caused by more valuable features.

WH5.3 The consideration of identifier attributes can have positive effects for error rates and model complexity.

WH5.4 Simple feature subset selection techniques can help to further accelerate learning after propositionalization and even improve accuracy. This potential originates from the opportunity that semantic-blind propositionalization produces many low-value features, which bear the danger to be misleading for learning.

WH5.5 Based on experience gained from earlier experiments, cf. Section 4.5, support-vector machine learning is expected to be *not* better than decision tree learning after propositionalization w.r.t. error rates and runtimes. Comprehensibility of the models is not a demand on support-vector machine learning, thus we do not focus on model complexity for SVMs here.

WH5.6 More complex features, here especially those based on conditional aggregation, cost more than learning from them returns.

5.4.2 Material

The material — data sets and learning tasks — are essentially the same as used above, cf. Section 4.5. For more details, including information about the new star schemas for those data, the reader is referred to Appendix B. For aspects of the software, please see Appendix A.

5.4.3 Procedure

We start from the same databases for the experiments with different propositionalizers and learners. Contrary to Section 4.5, these are *not* the reduced databases but the *original* databases in all cases. This is why we also report times for reducing databases here. All experiments are performed on the same platform for comparability especially of running times. We systematically vary the settings for the application of RELAGGS in the following way.

First, for the convenience of the reader, we repeat results achieved with RELAGGS earlier, cf. Section 4.5, now including database reduction times.

Second, we apply RELAGGS with the very same parameter settings, i.e. especially a restriction on the maximum cardinality of the sets of possible values of nominal attributes, to the same data, now in new star schemas. Aspects of the creation of new star schemas are also reported. Note that the feature sets produced here are subsets of those from the first experimental condition.

Third, we again apply RELAGGS with the same settings to the new star data, however, including the computation of more aggregate functions. For numeric data, we also consider *standard deviations* and *ranges*. For integer columns, we add *counts of distinct values, median*, and *1-/3-quartiles*. For nominal attributes, we also compute *counts of distinct values, relative frequencies of values*, and *modes*. Note that results of this kind of propositionalization are supersets of those from the second exerimental strain. There are overlaps with feature sets from the first part of the experiments. More exactly, the intersection of feature sets from series 1 and series 3 are exactly those from series 2.

Fourth, we apply RELAGGS as in step 3, but also consider identifier attributes, which were excluded so far. More precisely, in a well-controlled way, we include identifier attributes from other relations than the target relation. Those from the target relation could also be useful, but we focus on multi-relational learning and thus restrict our attention to the effect of identifiers from other relations. By "well-controlled", we mean that we investigate identifier attributes beforehand, if they have predictive potential in principle. So, the feature sets produced here are supersets of those created in step 3.

Fifth, to the RELAGGS results from step 3, we apply a WEKA attribute selector that ranks features by their information gain (IG). We then use only those features with an $IG > 0$ for propositional learning with both J48, a decision tree learning algorithm, and SMO, a support-vector machine learner. Obviously, feature sets here are subsets of those created in step 3. We use the IG attribute selector as a filter, because we had found it most efficient for our purposes in former experiments [72].

Last not least, we also conduct conditional aggregation. Here, data are grouped according to values of certain nominal attributes, before all the aggregate functions mentioned in step 3 are applied. This restricted aggregation is kept local to tables. That is why it has no effect for the narrow tables of the KRK, Mutagenesis and Gene problems. For the other learning tasks, special parameter settings are necessary in most cases in order to avoid the construction of tables that are too broad to be handled by MySQL. Hence, comparability with the other experiments is restricted. Nevertheless, we report a number of special results.

Table 5.2: Running times for propositionalization and WEKA learning (in seconds; non-std. — non-standard aggregate functions on new stars, fea.-sel. — feature selection on non-std.; two lines per learning task: time for propositionalization in first line, time for WEKA learning in second line, for training runs on all examples; n. a. cases explained in the main text)

Target	RELAGGS	New star	Non-std.	IDs	Fea.-sel.	SMO
Trains.bound	2	1	1	n. a.	1	1
	0	0	0		0	1
KRK.illegal	36	n. a.	45	n. a.	45	45
	36		39		29	537
Muta042.active	8	n. a.	11	n. a.	11	11
	1		1		0	1
Muta188.active	8	n. a.	12	n. a.	12	12
	1		2		1	2
Partner.class	3,577	228	352	459	352	352
	1,799	315	566	846	496	> 1 d
Household.class	2,198	139	218	310	218	218
	427	40	108	173	80	> 1 d
Loan.status	190	22	28	40	28	28
	12	3	5	7	1	4
Card.type	445	47	65	78	65	65
	5	1	2	3	0	7
Gene.growth	13	n. a.	18	n. a.	18	18
	6		21		6	18
Gene.nucleus	14	n. a.	17	n. a.	17	17
	6		23		9	15

5.4.4 Results

Table 5.2 shows the running times for the central parts of learning. For all columns, the propositional learner J48 is applied, except for the last column, where SMO is applied after feature selection, i. e. to the same input as that for J48 in the last column but one.

The meanings of "n. a." are the following here. Those in the new star column mean that the original database was already in this schema. Those in the IDs column for Trains.bound and KRK.prediction mean that the identifiers there were artificially introduced not independent of the target objects' class labels, while the nominal IDs for Gene problems are too many to be considered in the usual way here. Those in the SMO column mean that running times were too long with more than a day.

Table 5.3: Running times for database reduction, new star generation, and feature subset selection (in seconds; n. a. for reasons of database schema)

Target	RDB reduction	New star creation	Feature selection
Trains20.bound	n. a.	0	0
KRK.illegal	n. a.	n. a.	8
Muta042.active	n. a.	n. a.	1
Muta188.active	n. a.	n. a.	2
Partner.class	15	20	72
Household.class	8	13	40
Loan.status	16	15	2
Card.type	16	21	1
Gene.growth	n. a.	n. a.	2
Gene.nucleus	n. a.	n. a.	2

Table 5.3 shows running times for specific preparations of learning. Database reduction is applied as in Section 4.5, to include only data with relationships to the target objects. New star generation is applied to the original data in the way described above. Feature subset selection refers to the application of WEKA's attribute selector that used IG to rank features.

Table 5.4 shows the overall running times for learning, i. e. sums of times for database reduction or new star generation, if applicable, propositionalization and the application of WEKA tools, i. e. attribute selectors and learners.

Table 5.5 shows, for each of the experimental conditions, the average error across the partitions and the standard deviation. The best results are marked in **bold**.

Win-loss-tie statistics are provided in Table 5.6. Significance is determined according to a paired t-test at level $\alpha = 0.05$.

In Table 5.7, column numbers resulting from propositionalization are listed. They correspond to the number of attributes as used by WEKA.

In Table 5.8, the information gain is provided for the feature of each appropriate experimental condition that was ranked first by WEKA's corresponding attribute selector. The condition with feature selection is not mentioned here, because best features there are by design of the experiment the same as for the condition "Non-std.".

In Table 5.9, tree sizes for trees as learned from all training data are given as the numbers of all their nodes and the numbers of their leaf nodes.

We further achieved the following results with conditional aggregation.

We applied RELAGGS with the same parameter settings as above on new star data including non-standard aggregate functions. Now, we additionally used conditional aggregation for both numeric and nominal attributes. Thus the resulting

Table 5.4: Overall running times (in seconds; for training runs on all examples; sums include preparation times and feature selection times, if applicable)

Target	RELAGGS	New star	Non-std.	IDs	Fea.-sel.	SMO
Trains.bound	2	1	1	n. a.	1	2
KRK.illegal	72	n. a.	84	n. a.	82	590
Muta042.active	9	n. a.	12	n. a.	12	13
Muta188.active	9	n. a.	14	n. a.	15	16
Partner.class	5,443	553	938	1,325	940	> 1 d
Household.class	2,668	192	339	496	351	> 1 d
Loan.status	222	40	48	62	46	49
Card.type	480	69	88	102	87	94
Gene.growth	19	n. a.	39	n. a.	26	38
Gene.nucleus	20	n. a.	40	n. a.	28	34

Table 5.5: Error rate averages and standard deviations (in percent; best results in **bold**, second best in *italics*)

Target	RELAGGS	New star	Non-std.	IDs	Fea.-sel.	SMO
Trains.bound	**10.0**	**10.0**	**10.0**	n. a.	**10.0**	*20.0*
	± 31.6	± 31.6	± 31.6		± 31.6	± 25.8
KRK.illegal	27.7	n. a.	*23.1*	n. a.	*23.1*	**22.5**
	± 1.1		± 1.0		± 1.0	± 1.0
Muta042.active	**14.3**	n. a.	23.8	n. a.	*19.3*	21.8
	± 16.0		± 18.3		± 18.6	± 17.4
Muta188.active	*13.2*	n. a.	15.5	n. a.	13.3	**10.1**
	± 9.1		± 9.6		± 8.1	± 4.0
Partner.class	**2.5**	4.5	*4.4*	5.0	4.5	n. a.
	± 0.5	± 0.8	± 0.8	± 0.7	± 0.7	
Household.class	*7.1*	**6.2**	7.9	8.0	7.6	n. a.
	± 0.8	± 0.6	± 1.0	± 1.1	± 0.8	
Loan.status	7.2	8.6	7.3	**4.0**	*5.9*	8.8
	± 3.4	± 3.1	± 2.8	± 1.2	± 2.2	± 3.1
Card.type	11.8	*11.1*	11.1	**11.0**	11.8	12.8
	± 2.4	± 2.6	± 2.9	± 2.5	± 0.5	± 1.6
Gene.growth	*17.9*	n. a.	18.7	n. a.	18.4	**17.4**
	± 4.0		± 3.1		± 5.2	± 6.5
Gene.nucleus	15.0	n. a.	*14.6*	n. a.	15.0	**12.4**
	± 2.5		± 2.3		± 2.3	± 2.6

Table 5.6: Win-loss-tie statistics (row vs. column)

	New star	Non-std.	IDs	Fea.-sel.	SMO
RELAGGS	1–1–3	1–1–8	1–1–2	1–1–8	0–2–6
New star		1–0–3	1–1–2	1–1–3	0–0–3
Non-std. aggr.			0–1–3	0–1–9	0–0–8
Identifiers				1–0–3	1–0–1
Feature selection					2–1–5

Table 5.7: Numbers of columns in results of propositionalization

Target	RELAGGS	New star	Non-std.	IDs	Fea.-sel.
Trains.bound	57	35	83	n. a.	23
KRK.illegal	13	n. a.	30	n. a.	21
Muta042.active	483	n. a.	977	n. a.	51
Muta188.active	483	n. a.	977	n. a.	337
Partner.class	1,078	223	430	532	362
Household.class	1,197	232	466	606	349
Loan.status	1,021	217	452	557	74
Card.type	421	90	159	210	25
Gene.growth	200	n. a.	405	n. a.	120
Gene.nucleus	208	n. a.	421	n. a.	174

Table 5.8: Information gain for best-ranked features (best results in **bold**)

Target	RELAGGS	New star	Non-std.	IDs
Trains.bound	0.493	0.493	**0.698**	n. a.
KRK.illegal	0.024	n. a.	**0.135**	n. a.
Muta042.active	**0.474**	n. a.	**0.474**	n. a.
Muta188.active	**0.384**	n. a.	**0.384**	n. a.
Partner.class	0.293	0.198	0.201	**0.303**
Household.class	**0.570**	**0.570**	**0.570**	**0.570**
Loan.status	0.136	0.136	0.136	**0.258**
Card.type	**0.080**	**0.080**	**0.080**	**0.080**
Gene.growth	**0.151**	n. a.	**0.151**	n. a.
Gene.nucleus	0.148	n. a.	**0.199**	n. a.

Table 5.9: Tree sizes (number of nodes / number of leaves)

Target	RELAGGS	New star	Non-std.	IDs	Fea.-sel.
Trains.bound	5/3	5/3	5/3	n. a.	5/3
KRK.illegal	957/479	n. a.	231/116	n. a.	217/109
Muta042.active	9/5	n. a.	9/5	n. a.	5/3
Muta188.active	25/13	n. a.	17/9	n. a.	17/9
Partner.class	167/85	316/173	300/162	184/97	276/150
Household.class	290/175	375/302	284/211	301/217	280/206
Loan.status	31/16	20/11	33/17	15/8	25/13
Card.type	21/11	23/12	34/18	34/18	1/1
Gene.growth	67/35	n. a.	54/32	n. a.	23/12
Gene.nucleus	57/30	n. a.	32/17	n. a.	32/17

feature set is a superset for that of the third experimental condition above. RE-
LAGGS produced here for the Trains.bound problem a number of 493 features in
5 seconds, resulting in a 5/3 tree with an error rate of 15.0 % ± 24.2 %. Although
the average is below the best seen above, the standard deviation is reduced here,
which can be seen as a favorable effect. Feature selection found 74 features with
$IG > 0$, producing the same tree as above. SMO learning resulted in an error
rate of 20.0 % ± 25.8 %. All learning processes took less than 0.5 sec.

For Loan.status prediction, we had to lower the maximum allowed number of
possible values of nominal attributes down to 10 in order to arrive at result tables
from propositionalization that could be handled by MySQL. With this restriction,
RELAGGS produced a number of 773 features in 124 seconds, resulting in a 19/11
tree with an error rate of 7.3 % ± 3.7 %. Feature selection extracted 186 features
with $IG > 0$. After that, J48 learned a tree with 30/16 nodes in 3 sec, with an
error rate 6.2 % ± 2.3 %. After 43 sec, SMO learning resulted in an error rate
of 8.1 % ± 2.9 %, which is the best performance of SMO on this problem seen in
our experiments.

For Household.class prediction, the parameters had to be further adopted. On
the one hand, the same parameter settings could be applied as before, including
a value of 10 for the maximum allowed cardinality of sets of possible values
for nominal attributes. On the other hand, conditional aggregation could not
include aggregation of nominal attributes without producing too large tables and
exceeding main memory resources too much.

Furthermore, we had to restrict our attention to the 6 standard aggregate
functions as used for experiments in strains 1 and 2 above. The feature set
produced here is thus a superset of those produced under the second experimental
condition above. Results were the following. Without feature selection, J48
arrived at a 629/548 tree after 253 sec based on 1,100 features. The error rate

from stratified 10-fold cross-validation was 7.9 % ± 1.0 %, significantly worse than for the simple new star application.

With feature selection, 796 features remained, from which J48 learned a 404/319 tree within 197 sec, showing an error rate of 7.4 % ± 1.0 %, which is still significantly worse than in example strain 2 above, but significantly better than without feature selection. Feature selection took 99 sec, and the best ranked feature showed an IG of 0.57. The same feature was also produced in the other experiments. Follow-up features were produced by conditional aggregation, though.

Finally, we were able to reproduce results for RSD as reported in a paper on comparisons of approaches to propositionalization [65]. Especially, the short running time of only a couple of seconds using new star data should be mentioned, compared to more than 20 min as reported above, cf. special results for RSD in Section 4.5.

5.4.5   Discussion

From Table 5.2, we can see that the usage of data in a new star format is especially favorable for the efficiency of propositionalization. In many cases, the performance gain amounts to one order of magnitude. The gains for propositional learning are not as high, but distinct in a number of cases, resulting from the lower number of features that were produced. Thus, we can confirm WH5.1A from our experiments.

WH5.1B can also be confirmed, especially when considering Table 5.6. Here, most of the time differences in accuracy are marked as not significant.

However, WH5.1C can not be confirmed. As shown in Table 5.9, trees even grow occasionally for new star data. This may have to do with the information loss, i. e. loss of high-value features from joins including more than two tables, which have now to be replaced by more low-value features to arrive at a comparable tree performance.

When more aggregate functions are used, time gains reached with the usage of new star data get smaller. Although we see from Table 5.8, that some of the new features have occasionally higher IGs, the overall error rate after extended aggregation is not better than under the experimental conditions before. Tree sizes remain in the same order of magnitude. Overall, we do not see strong indicators for WH5.2A here.

WH5.2B is confirmed. There are still efficiency gains compared to not using new star data.

WH5.2C is not confirmed by our experiments. A reason for these results might be that the new aggregate functions are mostly similar in spirit to standard aggregate functions, such as the median compared to the average or the relative frequency of a nominal value compared to its absolute frequency.

Considering identifiers, we see just one favorable case, cf. Table 5.5. On closer inspection, the transaction identifiers for the PKDD financial data seem to encode both dates and certain types of transactions, which makes them expressive for the problem at hand. Note that the resulting models should be applied only to the other customers described in the database, i. e. those that have not yet a loan project running but might apply for it. However, the problem of applying data mining results to new data is a general one. We do not put it in our special focus here. We see WH5.3 as confirmed, but we are aware of the fact that results have to be handled with special care.

WH5.4 is not confirmed by our experiments, overall. Direct learning with WEKA tools is about as fast as first selecting features with IG > 0 and learning on the reduced feature sets. Also, occasional statistically significant wins are contrasted by about the same number of losses, which makes a general statement difficult. Remarkably, the number of features with IG > 0 is not as low as expected but in most cases in the same order of magnitude as the number of the features in the sets that were input to the selectors, cf. Table 5.7.

A surprise were the good results for SMO learning with 4 wins and 1 second rank, cf. Table 5.5. For Mutagenesis188, it is even the best result seen overall in our experiments, even slightly better than FOIL, although not significantly, cf. Section 4.5. As a rule, results for SMO after feature selection were the best seen for that learner.

Under a certain perspective, this even confirms the evaluation of SVM learning as strong in the presence of larger numbers of moderately relevant features [59]. Exactly selecting features with a certain correlation with the class labels might have produced such sets of moderately relevant features. Considering significances and running times, though, WH5.5 is confirmed.

WH5.6 is weakly confirmed. The effort to produce features by conditional aggregation is not outweighed by the occasionally interesting results. Still the low number of experiments and their diversity does not allow for a final judgement.

Especially, we mention the advantages of using databases in a new star schema for other ILP learners. For RSD, we saw efficiency gains exemplified before [65]. Similar effects can be expected for other ILP learners, e. g. for PROGOL.

We can also observe this as gains in effectivity: with the default parameter settings e. g. of RSD or PROGOL, all relations can be considered, which was frequently not the case without using new stars. Also, more relations can be considered within one clause of a certain length. Last not least, ease of use is improved with simpler mode declarations that are sufficient for learning here.

Finally, we emphasize ease of use of RELAGGS. In a base case, the user has only to specify the target relation or attribute, which he or she can see in a tree directly produced from relational database schema information, cf. Appendix A. There are few parameters to be set, which should be comprehensible for many analysts. An open problem for further work is an appropriate support for users in their choice of aggregate functions.

5.4.6   Further Related Work

Some related work was already mentioned in the early sections of this chapter, e.g. by Lavrač and Flach [77] on irrelevancy treatment. Here, we point to further related work.

Vens and colleagues [128] build up on ideas by Blockeel and Bruynooghe [13] and by Knobbe and colleagues [55], cf. Subsection 4.5.6. The authors present an approach to learn special first-order trees, including the usage of aggregate functions of different kinds.

Interestingly, the authors [128] find simple aggregate functions as used within the basic variant of RELAGGS as almost as useful as more complex aggregate functions, which include selections in the spirit of conditional aggregation as presented in this chapter. Our results support these findings w.r.t. effectiveness. Concerning efficiency, the authors aim at improvements by future work.

Similar ideas as ours for new star schemas can be found in different resources. For instance, Dehaspe and De Raedt [27] assume a database where all relations have exactly one attribute that corresponds to the key of examples, i.e. each non-target table has a foreign key attribute pointing to the primary key attribute of the target table. However, the authors do not focus on the generation of such databases.

Yin and colleagues [137] report on their system CROSSMINE, which also exploits propagated identifiers of target objects. Different from our approach, propagation is done here during relational rule learning in the spirit of FOIL. Moreover, class labels are propagated along with identifiers. First experimental results are promising.

For his Master's thesis, Reutemann [109] adopted RELAGGS as a preprocessing tool for WEKA and applied it to a number of learning tasks and in comparison to other approaches for relational learning. Overall, RELAGGS turned out to have favorable characteristics in those experiments.

Finally, we would like to point the interested reader to other current research in the field of propositionalization, initiated by Železný. He provides further perspectives on issues of propositionalization and more detailed complexity analyses, especially for further developments of the traditional approaches [129, 130].

5.5   Summary

We presented an approach for transforming usual RDB schemas into new star schemas, which can serve as a basis for efficient propositionalization and other methods of relational learning. We discussed the treatment of RDB that induce cyclic undirected graphs, where human intervention seems advisable. Further, we showed that there is no information loss involved in new star generation, and that materialized views are a good option for the implementation of new star databases. Moreover, we demonstrated that new star databases are superior to universal relations for our purposes.

We then introduced more aggregate functions into our method for propositionalization and motivated the inclusion of primary key attributes of non-target tables into analyses. As post-processing for results of propositionalization, we considered different approaches to both feature selection and feature construction.

Our empirical evaluation showed significant gains in efficiency from using databases in a new star schema. Positive effects of new aggregate functions, especially more complex functions using selections, were not as large as expected. Simple feature selection methods had favorable effects on error rates and model complexity in a number of cases.

Chapter 6

Conclusions and Future Work

In conclusion, we condense the answers to the general research questions posed in the introductory chapter of this thesis.

1. Approaches to propositionalization can be described in a unified way within a formal framework. We showed that with our presentation of transformation functions on results of clauses as queries to relational data including background knowledge.

2. Aggregate functions tailored to data types of attributes can serve as a part of such transformations in an especially favorable way. Their results are not only a basis for effective KDD in many cases, but also efficient to compute and easy to apply.

3. Further measures building up on database technologies, e. g. special schema transformations of databases using indexing, can further increase efficiency significantly, while not sacrificing the quality of learning results.

Overall, propositionalization was shown to be a valuable approach to relational data mining and competitive with prominent systems from Inductive Logic Programming. Being often similarly effective but much more efficient, and furthermore easy to use, propositionalization could be the preferred approach, especially for the analysis of larger business data sets.

During our work presented in this thesis, there remained or appeared a number of open questions that could be dealt with in future work.

Although our framework was shown to largely fulfil the expectations formulated for them, also for extensions of existing approaches to propositionalization in a systematic way, we see opportunities to further refine the framework. Building blocks for propositionalization could be elaborated and serve as a basis for more concise descriptions of the single approaches, thus also enabling a faster comparison during human inspection and more detailed analyses of computational complexities.

Beside this more general issue, there are many more special research questions, some of which we enumerate in the following.

- Could a search procedure in the space of aggregate functions, which should be applied during propositionalization, be designed and implemented successfully? Which aggregate functions reach good points in the effectivity vs. efficiency spectrum, e.g. *counts* of possible nominal value v vs. *exists* possible value v?

- Would it be favorable to compute estimates of *cost vs. benefit* for the inclusion of non-target relations into propositionalization? Should the granularity for these considerations be increased to evaluate attributes or even single values of attributes within those relations?

- Can intuitions be confirmed that the relevance of non-target relations for the quality of learning task solutions depends on their distance to the target relation? Would that allow for strategies such as "breadth-first propositionalization"?

- If there are several paths in the graph induced by an RDB leading from the target relation to another relation: can recommendations be made to choose from the different opportunities to deal with such a situation? One may assume that simple options should be tried first, e.g. using (one of) the shortest path(s) only.

- Are there more efficient ways to compute aggregate function values? For instance, should certain values such as *ranges* be computed only after propositionalization, which included the computation of *maxima* and *minima* as a basis for *range* computation in the style of conventional feature construction? Which functions would be appropriate here?

- How can irrelevant features be treated efficiently, i.e. at best their generation avoided?

- Which features resulting from complex propositionalization operators could be simulated by simpler ones? Which propositional learners should be preferred and why? Are there dependencies on characteristics of original data sets, learning tasks, or results of propositionalization?

- How should imperfect input data be dealt with, such as wrong data, outliers, missing values, too few data points? Some aggregate functions such as *median* seem appropriate to avoid or at least alleviate some effects, e.g. of outliers.

- Are there promising features that can be produced exclusively within certain approaches to propositionalization, e. g. traditional or supervised propositionalization? Are there features that can be computed especially efficiently within one kind of approaches compared to others? Could there be thus opportunities to favorably combine approaches? Could good features from propositionalization be used to enrich hypotheses determined with ILP systems?

- There were investigations if ILP systems such as PROGOL can cope without attributes developed by domain experts, by using complex and intensional background knowledge instead. Similarly, one might ask if propositionalization in the style of RELAGGS can cope without PROGOL's kind of background knowledge, by using simpler structured and extensional background knowledge.

With more, more diverse and larger relational databases for analyses to be expected available in the future, we hope for interesting further developments in the area of research, both in general for relational data mining, and especially for propositionalization.

Appendix A

Software

In this appendix, we provide short descriptions of software tools that were used for our experiments. All software tools developed by the author and colleagues are available on request for non-commercial purposes from the author. Other software that we used is also freely available in many cases, most under GNU public license. For a description of the hardware, cf. Section 4.5.

The central program for our experiments is RELAGGS. We applied the latest version which was implemented by Körnig for his diploma thesis [57] under the author's supervision in autumn 2004. It is an extended reimplementation of the program that was developed by Streuer [124] as part of her term project in 2002/2003, which was used for earlier experiments [65, 74].

That program in turn was based on other work by our students, which was the first implementation using Java for the application program and MySQL for the management of the databases [112, 113] . The original version was developed by the author in a Prolog environment and used for our first experiments in the field [71] as well as for KDD Cup 2001 [22].

The latest version of RELAGGS is illustrated in the following with a number of screenshots. These are taken in a Windows environment because of their better appearance there. Figure A.1 shows the window for parameter settings that can be modified before connecting to a database for propositionalization. The figure shows the default settings which were used in most of the experiments here, except that we did not demand nominal values to occur for a certain percentage of the learning examples. Further explanations may be found in the system's documentation.

Figure A.2 shows the main window of RELAGGS displaying a selected database with its table and attribute names. Color codes indicate primary keys, targets, as well as objects excluded from propositionalization by the user. Also, numeric or nominal attributes may be excluded from the investigations separately.

Figure A.3 presents the part of the main window of RELAGGS where a subset of aggregate functions can be selected by the user. The selections made for our experiments can be found in the main text of Sections 4.5 and 5.4.

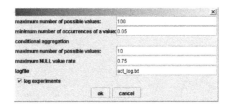

maximum number of possible values:	100
minimum number of occurrences of a value:	0.05
conditional aggregation	
maximum number of possible values:	10
maximum NULL value rate	0.75
logfile	act_log.txt
✓ log experiments	

Figure A.1: The RELAGGS window for settings

Figure A.4 depicts the part of the main window of RELAGGS where a name
for the result table, which will be stored in the same database, can be provided by
the user and propositionalization can be started. A progress bar informs about
the state of the process.

With these means, a tool for propositionalization is given which we found
comfortable to use.

For the export of propositionalization result tables from MySQL to the format used by WEKA, the author implemented a tool called Arffer, again in Java.
Figure A.5 shows a screenshot. Arffer offers options that go beyond the corresponding export function within RELAGGS. Documentation is included in the
release version.

Another tool called CVPartiNicer was implemented by the author, among
others based on ideas by our students from their term projects under the author's supervision. It splits ARFF data files into partitions for stratified cross-
validation, cf. Figure A.6. Both the number of partitions and a seed for the
random number generator can be provided by the user. We worked with the
default settings as shown in the figure.

We simulated DINUS with the help of RELAGGS by simply excluding all relations different from the target relation and those tables with a many-to-one
relationship from the target relation to them. The simulation of ROLLUP was
also achieved with RELAGGS by iteratively propositionalizing along one-to-many
relationships and simple joins along many-to-one relationships, starting from the
relation(s) most distant from the target relation.

For PROGOL, inputs were produced from MySQL database tables with the
help of one more tool written by the author and called Progoler, cf. Figure A.7.
Since it deals only with single tables, a certain amount of manual adaptations of
the Progol input files has to be carried out by the user. Also, a program for the
support of cross-validation was derived from the one mentioned above and called
CVPartiNicerP.

For the application of RSD, we used our tool ProgolToRSD for a rewrite of
the examples, and ProgolToRSDb for a rewrite of the mode declarations. This
rewrite seemed a good idea considering the minor differences between the input

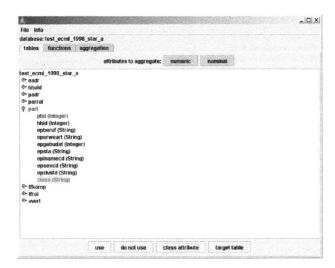

Figure A.2: The RELAGGS main window part for database inspection and learning task definition

formats of the two systems in question.

Analogous to PROGOL, we created and applied tools in preparation of the runs of FOIL and TILDE, viz. tools called Foiler and Tilder, and CVPartiNicerF and CVPartiNicerT. Again, all our tools are available on request for non-commercial use from the author.

Finally, we provide the version numbers of software from other sources that we used. Current versions should be easily located on the Web.

- Solaris 9 (SunOS 5.9)

- Java 1.4.2

- JDBC mysql-connector-java-3

- MySQL 4.0.21

- YAP 4.4

- WEKA 3.4

- FOIL 6

- PROGOL 5.0 (CProgol)

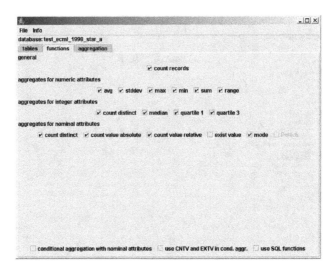

Figure A.3: The RELAGGS main window part for aggregate function selection

- TILDE 2.2 within ACE-ilProlog 1.2.6-huge
- RSD 1.0

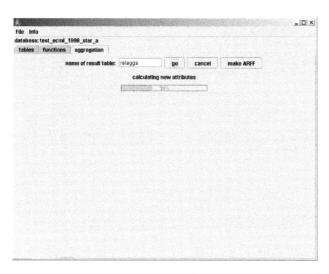

Figure A.4: The RELAGGS main window part for the start of propositionalization

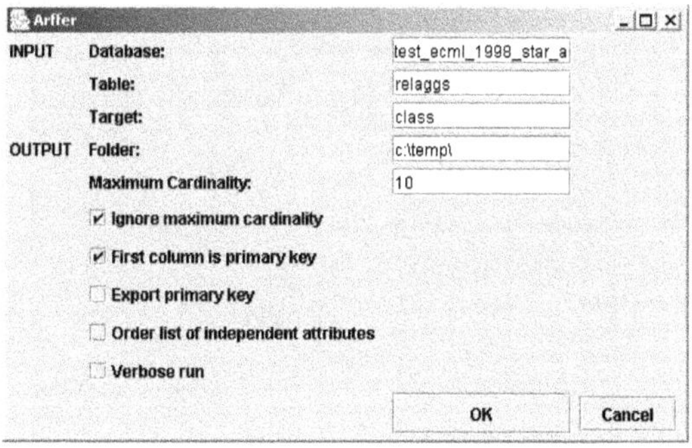

Figure A.5: A tool for exporting a MySQL table into an ARFF file

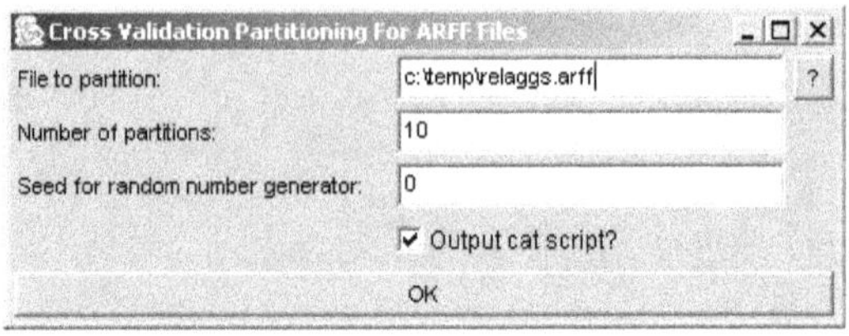

Figure A.6: A tool for partitioning an ARFF file for stratified n-fold cross-validation

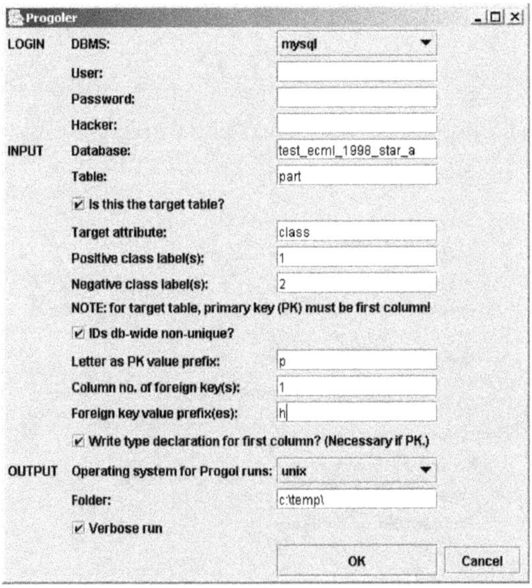

Figure A.7: A tool for exporting a MySQL table into files with Progol input format

Appendix B

Data Sets and Learning Tasks

The main objective of this appendix is to enable the reader to repeat the experiments as easily as possible. For this reason, we provide

- information about the sources of the data sets for our experiments

- short descriptions of the data sets

- short descriptions of the learning tasks for the experiments

- descriptions of details of the preparation of the data sets for the usage of the different systems applied for the experiments

- short descriptions of special circumstances, if applicable

Files documenting the single steps of the procedure, SQL scripts, their log files, and tools such as for producing different formats of the data set from MySQL tables or for the preparation of stratified cross-validation are available from the author on request. We can also provide the databases, inputs, logs, and outputs of the experiments.

Certain restrictions apply w.r.t. ECML and PKDD challenge data, though. For ECML data, third parties have to be asked for permission. For PKDD data, challenge organizers should be informed.

Note that most of the learning problems were subjects of earlier experiments of ours [71, 67]. However, specifics in the preparation of the data sets and in the settings for the learning systems cause differences between the results. We worked with the learning task for Card.type here for the first time.

We describe the preparation of the data for the application of the different learning systems in most detail for the PKDD 1999/2000 Challenge financial data set, especially for task Loan.status. This has to do with the specifics of these data and task. For instance, the number of tables and their relationships allows for observing interesting aspects not to be seen for less complex tasks such as for Trains.bound or KRK.illegal, on the one hand. Loan.status also allows

135

for describing preparations rather completely, which would be difficult here for more complex problems such as for Partner.class or Household.class, on the other hand.

B.1 Challenge 1994: Trains.bound

Trains data sets and learning tasks belong to the standard problems in Machine Learning and Inductive Logic Programming.

The data source we used is

ftp://ftp.comlab.ox.ac.uk/pub/Packages/ILP/Trains/20trains.pl

This data set was used for competition 1 in the East-West Challenge [83]. A subset of the 20 trains, which is the original 10 trains problem as formulated by Michalski [81] is depicted in Figure B.1.

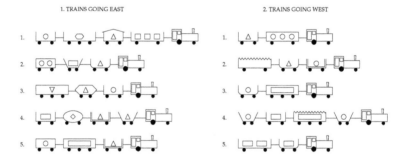

Figure B.1: The ten trains East-West Challenge [81, 77]

The original data are structured facts such that identifier attributes are not necessary. For instance, the first train is described as follows:

```
eastbound([c(1,rectangle,short,not_double,none,2,l(circle,1)),
           c(2,rectangle,long,not_double,none,3,l(hexagon,1)),
           c(3,rectangle,short,not_double,peaked,2,l(triangle,1)),
           c(4,rectangle,long,not_double,none,2,l(rectangle,3))]).
```

This means, according to the documentation for the East-West Challenge, that the first train is eastbound and has four cars, the first of which is in position

1, of rectangular shape and short length, has "not-double" walls, no roof and two (times two) wheels, further a load of circle shape, one piece.

From those data, we produced a relational database with three tables, where each train, car, and load has an integer identifier. Actually, load information could have been added directly to the car relation because of the one-to-one relationship between cars and loads in the data. However, we decided to remain close to the original representation here.

For the same reason, we did not use a different schema for the loads table, e. g. with one entry per piece, which would have allowed for load pieces of different shape within one car. Actually, preliminary experiments in this scenario showed good results.

Choices of types numeric and nominal for the attributes are obvious here.

train			car									load			
t_id	bound		c_id	t_id	posi	shape	length	wall	roof	wheels		l_id	c_id	shape	number
1	east		1	1	1	rect	short	single	none	2		1	1	circle	1
2	east		2	1	2	rect	long	single	none	3		2	2	hexa	1
...	...		...	...	...	...	...	...	...	...		...	...	...	...

Figure B.2: A relational database for trains (relations as structured rectangles with their names in the first lines, attribute names in the second lines, and attribute values below; arrows represent foreign key relationships)

The learning task asks for a model to classify trains into those bound east and those bound west. There are 50 % representatives of each class in the data.

The systems FOIL, PROGOL, TILDE, and RSD use the database in their corresponding formats. For RELAGGS in its base version, cf. Chapter 4, a join of the car and load relations was precomputed. For the new star version, the trains identifiers were propagated to the loans relation.

A minor issue that could be observed during data preparation was the fact that some inconsistencies appeared even in this small data set. In a small number of cases, the number of loads was given in the original data as 0, while there was still a shape for this "non-load" provided. We did not change these aspects, though, in order to arrive at results that can be better compared with those of other research.

A variant of the data set can be found in the UCI Machine Learning Repository [11], occasionally named INDUCE Trains Data set. Interestingly, this is a manually propositionalized variant including Boolean attributes such as *rectangle_next_to_rectangle*, thus demonstrating the wide range of propositionalization functions.

B.2   Chess: KRK.illegal

The King-Rook-King (KRK) problem of classifying chess endgame situations is one of the ILP standard problems and was originally used for investigations with the system GOLEM [89].

We used as the source for the data

`ftp://ftp.comlab.ox.ac.uk/pub/Packages/ILP/Datasets/chess/`

According to the file Readme.ps to be found there, examples are described with the help of the predicate *illegal/6*, where the arguments stand for the file and rank of the white king, the white rook, and the black king, respectively. Figure B.3 shows two examples from the data set documentation. The example on the left would be described by *illegal(e,3,a,1,e,1)*, while the example on the right would be described by *not(illegal(d,4,g,3,b,5))*.

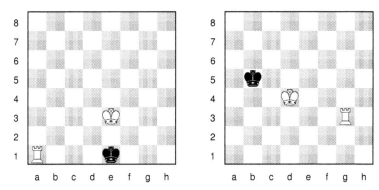

Figure B.3: Two chess situations

Further, two predicates are provided as background knowledge: *lt/2*, which contains facts to describe which file/rank is less than another, and *adj/2*, which records pairs of adjacent file/rank values. Note that this is background knowledge in a narrow sense: it is independent of the learning examples, i.e. positions of the three figures on the board.

However, it seems not obvious that exactly these two predicates are necessary and sufficient to solve learning tasks here. Moreover, it seems questionable if relations such as these would usually be found in relational databases in the form of explicit relations, instead of being computed on demand by the application program, for instance.

The learning task aims at a classifier to distinguish illegal from legal situations. There are 20,000 examples, among them 6,601 positive for the illegal case.

Actually, in the original data letters for file values are also replaced by numbers. Still, the original problem shows limits of the RELAGGS approach.

First, the construction of a normalized database seems not straightforward. It could be imagined by introducing a table that contains the distinct file/rank values as a primary key, with the columns from *illegal*, *adj* and *lt* as foreign key attributes. We did not use this somewhat artificial variant.

Second, for simulating the effect of, say, *adj* directly on *illegal*, RELAGGS would have to include literals for $X = Y$, $X = Y - 1$, and $X = Y + 1$ in its clauses for $\mathcal{C}$. However, this would cause an explosion of $\mathcal{C}$ in the general case, at least as long as only numeric and nominal types are differentiated. This differentiation is typical and intended for RELAGGS. For these reasons, we designed a new database schema as described in the following.

For our experiments, we designed a database following the considerations on the kind of background knowledge above. Here, we use a target table called *situation* with two columns: an identifier for a situation and a class attribute. Further, we define a second table describing parts of the situation. More precisely, this table has an identifier for the part, a foreign key to the situation identifier, an attribute for the name of the figure concerned, one attribute for its file, and one attribute for its rank, cf. Figure B.4. Thus there are three rows in the part table for each situation.

With this schema, it is simple to describe any chess situation, not only those involving the kings and a white rook. The information from the original *illegal* predicate is preserved completely this way, while we do not use *adj* and *lt*. This schema also fulfills the new star schema demands, cf. Chapter 5. Thus, there is no further special preprocessing necessary for the application of both the base variant and the extended variants of RELAGGS. The database was also directly used to derive the input files for the other systems we experimented with.

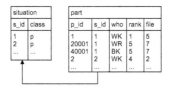

Figure B.4: A relational database for chess boards (relations as structured rectangles with their names in the first lines, attribute names in the second lines, and attribute values below; arrow represents foreign key relationship)

Table B.1: Relations of the Mutagenicity data set (target relations in **bold**)

No.	Relation	# ID attr.	# nominal attr.	# numeric attr.
1	anthracene	1	1	0
2	atm	1	3	1
3	ball3	1	1	0
4	benzene	1	1	0
5	bond	1	3	0
6	carbon_5_aromatic_ring	1	1	0
7	carbon_6_ring	1	1	0
8	**drug042/drug188**	1	1	0
9	hetero_aromatic_5_ring	1	1	0
10	hetero_aromatic_6_ring	1	1	0
11	logp	1	0	1
12	lumo	1	0	1
13	methyl	1	1	0
14	nitro	1	1	0
15	methyl	1	1	0
16	phenanthrene	1	1	0
17	ring_size_5	1	1	0
18	ring_size_6	1	1	0

B.3   Biochemistry: Mutagenesis042/188.active

Learning tasks in the field of mutagenicity modelling belong to the ILP standard problems. We used as a source for the data:

http://web.comlab.ox.ac.uk/oucl/research/areas/machlearn/mutagenesis.html

The data describe certain molecules. Table B.1 shows the predicates or relations the facts of which were used for our experiments. The first column enumerates the predicates, the second provides their names. The numbers of identifier attributes, of nominal attributes, and of numeric attributes follow in columns 3, 4, and 5, respectively.

The relations drug042/drug188 are derived from the original predicate *active* for 42 regression-unfriendly and 188 regression-friendly example descriptions, cf. descriptions of the data set [123]. The constellation given here corresponds largely to the usage of non-structural attributes (logp and lumo) and the structural attribute set S2 from experiments with PROGOL [123], also known in the literature as the variant with background knowledge B4 [54]. Indicator attributes, also called PS (ind1, inda), are not used here in correspondence with other work [123].

We use two learning tasks as indicated by the two names for target relations, also in correspondence with other work in the field. The objective is to arrive at models for the mutagenicity of drugs.

There are occasionally one-to-one relationships between the target relation and other relations, though in most cases there are one-to-many (many includes zero) relationships.

The identifier attributes are primary keys for the target relations, and foreign keys pointing to the target relation in all other cases. Thus, the database fulfills the demands of a new star schema.

The nominal attributes often consist of lists of (lists of) Prolog constants to describe certain structures of the molecules. We excluded drug identifiers here such that several drugs may share nominal values.

The transformation of the original Prolog facts to MySQL database tables was partly achieved with a Java tool named PL2SQL written by the author and available on request.

B.4   ECML Challenge 1998: Partner and Household.class

The data set as used for our experiments is not available in the Internet. We received it from Jörg-Uwe Kietz, who also distributed the data with a description of the data set in preparation of the Sisyphus-I workshop at the European Conference on Machine Learning (ECML) in 1998. Originally, the data were an excerpt of a data warehouse at the SwissLife insurance company. A new variant of the data was dealt with lately [86], conditions for the availability of those data is not known to the author.

Figure B.5 depicts parts of a relational database schema provided for the ECML 1998 challenge [52]. For the original tasks A and B of the challenge, there were two more tables included, both with a one-to-one-relationship to table *part* and to table *hhold*, respectively. They only contained partner and household identifiers, respectively, plus class labels. These were directly integrated into the tables *part* and *hhold*, respectively, for our experiments.

Table B.2 shows more details of the original relations.

The data describe partners (*part*) of the insurance companies, most of them customers, with their households (*hhold*) and addresses (*eadr* and *padr*), and their insurance contracts (*parrol*, *tfkomp*, *tfrol*, *vvert*).

For both learning tasks, the documentation explained that a value of 1 would be a positive class label, and 2 a negative class label, while a value of 0 would indicate an irrelevant case. The meaning of the learning tasks was not provided.

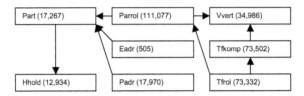

Figure B.5: The ECML 1998 challenge data set (relations as rectangles with
relation names and tuple numbers in parantheses; arrows represent foreign key
relationships [52])

Table B.2: Relations of the ECML 1998 challenge data set (target relations in
bold, target attributes indicated by "+1")

No.	Relation	# ID attr.	# nominal attr.	# numeric attr.
1	eadr	1	2	0
2	**hhold**	1	42+1	0
3	padr	1	3	0
4	parrol	3	2	0
5	**part**	2	6+1	1
6	tfkomp	3	10	13
7	tfrol	3	4	1
8	vvert	2	11	5

The focus of the challenge was on data preparation, and the small number of
contributions seems to indicate that the task was hard [9, 34, 52]. It is still
challenging as our experiments show.

We built a reduced database by dropping examples with class label 0. Further
preprocessing steps were analogous to those described in more detail for the
PKDD 1999/2000 Challenges below. Some special cirumstances here were the
following.

Many integer attributes were in fact nominal attributes, viz. codes for other
strings that are kept in other tables of the original data warehouse in several
languages used in Switzerland (French, German, Italian).

The many-to-many relationship between *part* and *vvert* via *parrol* included
several occurrences of the same *part-vvert*-pairs and thus made a `select distinct`
statement favorable when propagating target identifiers.

Further, *tfkomp* entries that can be reached via *vvert* are a real superset
of those reachable via *tfrol*, hence the decision to use only the first path for
propositionalization.

Last not least, there were a number of small deviations observed between the documentation of the data set and the actual state of it. Also, there were some attributes included showing only one value. Date values were taken here as integers in order to be included in the data mining process.

B.5   PKDD Challenge 1999: Loans and Cards

One of the two data sets provided for the PKDD Challenge in 1999 and also that in 2000 originates from a Czech bank and is also referred to in the literature as "financial data set". An introduction [8] and many interesting papers written by participants can be found in the internet, as well as the data:

`http://lisp.vse.cz/challenge/`

The data describe customers of the bank with their accounts, loans, orders and other transactions on those accounts, also their credit cards and aspects of the regions where customers and bank branches are situated.

Figure B.6 depicts parts of the relational database schema provided for the PKDD 1999/2000 challenges [8].

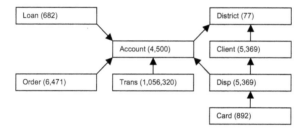

Figure B.6: The PKDD 1999/2000 challenges financial data set (relations as rectangles with relation names and tuple numbers in parantheses; arrows represent foreign key relationships [8])

Table B.3 shows more details of the original relations.

For the Challenge, learning tasks were not specified. However, several tasks turned out to be popular among the participants. Among those tasks were the prediction of the status of loan projects. Also, descriptions of phenomena w. r. t. the usage of credit cards were often an objective of data mining, e. g. for different types of credit cards. We concentrate on exactly these two tasks. Loan.status prediction is motivated by the hope to enable better decisions on granting loans. Card.type descriptions may help to upgrade some customers, ultimatly for better profit.

Table B.3: Relations of the PKDD 1999/2000 challenges financial data set (target relations in **bold**)

No.	Relation	# ID attr.	# nominal attr.	# numeric attr.
1	account	2	1	1
2	**card**	2	1	1
3	client	2	0	1
4	disp	3	1	0
5	district	1	2	13
6	**loan**	2	1	4
7	order	2	3	1
8	trans	2	5	3

As a first step for us to take, original data were imported into a MySQL database. Here, there are a number of choice points. For instance, data types have to be chosen, which is flexible within certain limits. Also, there is usually more than one way of defining key attributes, e. g. with or without explicit declarations of foreign key attributes, to allow for missing values or not, and for several other aspects of the database schema.

Many of these issues are related to efficiency, which is in general better for not nullable attributes, further for attributes of minimum type, say `char(2)` instead of `varchar(8)` or `tinyint` instead of `bigint`. However, determination of the applicability of restrictions can also be costly here. We decided the issues in pragmatic ways, aiming at simple and unified schemas.

We tried to keep the original names for tables and attributes to simplify handling of the databases, although occasionally deviations from this principle were necessary, e. g. for table *order_*, where `order` is a reserved word in MySQL.

Also, we observed small differences between the documentation of the data and the actual data, e. g. incomplete listings of possible values in the documentation, but also probably typos in the database. One attribute in the original customer table contained an attribute which combined information about birthday and gender. Here, we separated this information into two attributes.

Moreover, we had to manipulate values such as for Card.issued, which provided integers in strings for dates, but followed by 00:00:00. We removed the latter. Another observation concerned a deviation from the principle to have the same names for primary key attributes and their foreign key attributes in the original data. While foreign keys to the district table were named *district_id*, obviously following certain naming conventions here, the primary key attribute in the district table was named *A1*. These aspects exemplify the necessity for human intervention in the data preparation phase.

Data import into MySQL was achieved mainly with MySQL's `load data infile` command. It was highly efficient. For instance, more than one million transaction records could be imported from a text file into a MySQL table in less than a minute with that command, cf. Appendix C. Replacing empty strings or strings of spaces in the database by NULL values was also a fast achievement. Using text editors, the same task took three times as long.

Since further steps of data preparation were task specific, we present these separately in the following subsections.

B.5.1 Predicting Loan.status

For the first learning task considered here, table *loan* served as the target relation and its attribute *status* as the target attribute. This attribute has originally four different values with the following meanings.

- value A: loan project finished without problems

- value B: loan project finished with problems

- value C: loan project running, without problems so far

- value D: loan project running, with problems already

Problems could be delays or incomplete payback.

Following ideas of participants in the challenge, we combined examples of classes A and C into a positive class and those of classes B and D into a negative class. This way, we arrived not only at a two-class problem, but also at a moderate number of examples of 682. 606 of those loan projects had shown no problems. The models to be learned can be applied to each of those customers described by the database without a loan project at the point of time the database snapshot was taken.

Preprocessing Variant: Basic

In order to arrive at a reduced variant of the database, we deleted all entries without a relation to loans from the tables different from the target table. Furthermore, it was very important within the context of our prediction task to also leave out all data that dated after loan grantings, e. g. "late" transaction records. These data were not known at the time of granting loans such that comparable data would not be known for other customers who apply for a loan either.

This reduced variant of the database was taken as the basis for input production for the learning systems FOIL, PROGOL, TILDE, and RSD. It was also the starting point for further preparations of the data for the application of the basic variant of RELAGGS. For the latter, we defined foreign links in the usual way as first shown for MIDOS [133]. They correspond to foreign key relationships, but their direction may differ because foreign links always form directed paths from the target relation to the other relations. Furthermore, in the graph of the database with its foreign links, no circles are allowed. Figure B.7 depicts the database after reductions and with foreign link definitions. Note especially the reduction achieved for table *trans*.

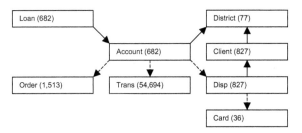

Figure B.7: The PKDD 1999/2000 challenges financial data set: reduced to relevant data for loan status prediction (solid arrows represent foreign links identical to former foreign key relationships, dashed arrows represent foreign links with a direction different from that of their basic foreign key relationship)

Following our ideas of exploiting functional dependencies between entries in different relations, we combined tables along many-to-one relationships. The resulting database is sketched in Fig. B.7

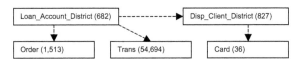

Figure B.8: The PKDD 1999/2000 challenges financial data set: after schema transformation exploiting functional dependencies (arrows represent foreign links)

In this situation, there are 12 clauses resulting to form $\mathcal{C}$, here represented by the predicate names of the literals only, i. e. without arguments.

1. loan_account_district

2. loan_account_district, disp_client_district

3. loan_account_district, order

4. loan_account_district, trans

5. loan_account_district, disp_client_district, card

6. loan_account_district, disp_client_district, order

7. loan_account_district, disp_client_district, trans

8. loan_account_district, order, trans

9. loan_account_district, disp_client_district, card, order

10. loan_account_district, disp_client_district, card, trans

11. loan_account_district, disp_client_district, order, trans

12. loan_account_district, disp_client_district, card, order, trans

A clause consisting of three literals for *loan_account_district*, *order*, and *card* is not included, since there would be no link to *card*; similar for some other cases.

With parameter branching factor set to 0, the subset of the first five clauses named above remains for $\mathcal{C}$. In our experiments for the basic variant of RELAGGS, we used exactly this set of clauses, where we produced their result sets in the database. This way, we arrived at new star formats, which enabled the simulation of the basic approach with the help of the same system as used for the extended variants. Running times for the transformations are included in the report on the empirical results, cf. Section 5.4.

Preprocessing Variant: New Star Schema

The propagation of loan identifiers was achieved corresponding to our suggestions for a general procedure for identifier propagation. This process also reduced the data in a similar way to that taken for the basic variant. Database entries dating after loan grantings had to be deleted in addition to the usual procedure, cf. Appendix C.

Figure B.9 depicts the database in a new star schema. Note that table *district* has grown here. This is caused by two reasons. First, we use the union of results from using two paths to the *district* table from the *loan* table: directly via *account*, and in addition via *client*. Second, denormalization introduced redundancies, e. g. when for two loans on accounts in the same district, district information is stored twice.

During new star generation, an order by target identifiers could have been produced, which could have been later exploited by RELAGGS. However, this step was not taken yet. Instead, RELAGGS produces the corresponding orders. It would be favorable to precompute those orders in cases of repeated propositionalization, say with different parameter settings or using different subsets of the aggregate functions available.

Also, we did not yet propagate class labels along with identifiers, which would allow for supervised propositionalization of the single tables involved.

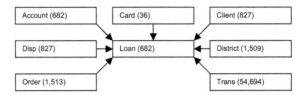

Figure B.9: The PKDD 1999/2000 challenges financial data set: database in a new star schema (arrows represent foreign key relationships)

B.5.2 Describing Card.type

For the second learning task derived from the PKDD 1999/2000 Challenges financial data set, we use table *card* as target relation and its attribute *type* as target attribute. Originally, this attribute has three values: *classic*, *gold*, and *junior*. Since *junior* was observed for a small group of young customers only, we left those credit cards out of our considerations.

A description of card usage may especially enable marketing attempts to upgrade classic card users with a similar profile as gold card users. There were 659 classic cards and 88 gold cards described in the target table, i. e. 747 examples overall to be considered.

The procedure for preprocessing was mainly analogous to the one described for the Loan.status learning task. We produced a reduced version of the database by leaving out those with no relationship to cards. This time, there are not any further restrictions such as those induced by dates, since we do not aim at predictive models but descriptive ones. We defined foreign links and exploited functional dependencies. This way, 8 clauses resulted for $\mathcal{C}$:

1. card_disp_account_district_client

2. card_disp_account_district_client, loan

3. card_disp_account_district_client, order

4. card_disp_account_district_client, trans

5. card_disp_account_district_client, loan, order

6. card_disp_account_district_client, loan, trans

7. card_disp_account_district_client, order, trans

8. card_disp_account_district_client, loan, order, trans

Table B.4: Relations of the KDD Cup 2001 gene data set (target relation in **bold**)

No.	Relation	# ID attr.	# nominal attr.	# numeric attr.
1	**gene**	1	6+2	0
2	interaction	2	1	1

With branching factor set to 0, the first 4 of those clauses were finally used for the application of RELAGGS in the basic scheme.

Preprocessing for the new star schema variant was done according to the general procedure.

B.6   KDD Cup 2001: Gene.growth and nucleus

For the KDD Cup 2001 [22, 70], three tasks were provided, the two latter of which dealt with yeast genes and the proteins they code for, respectively. Data, tasks and further documentation can be downloaded from

`http://www.cs.wisc.edu/~dpage/kddcup2001/`

The data describe genes/proteins: if they are essential for life of the cell or organism, on which chromosome the gene can be found, the protein's function(s) and localization. Further, protein class, complex, phenotype and motif information is provided. Moreover, interactions between proteins are recorded with their kind and strength. Table B.4 shows more details of the original relations.

The two tables per training and test data set in the original data were produced by denormalizing an unpublished database with more tables.

Task 2 of the KDD Cup 2001 asked for models to predict n functions out of 13 contained in the training data, for each protein. Task 3 demanded for models to predict *one* localization out of 15 contained in the training data, for each protein. There were 861 training examples given, with function and localization information, and 381 test examples without that information.

We decided to remain close to the original tasks with our experiments here. However, we concentrated on predicting just one specific function and one specific localization. For these, we chose the function and localization values that were closest to a fifty-fifty distribution among the examples. We expected to see the effects of learning most clearly here. The function value of interest included responsibility for cell growth, given for 275 of 861 training examples. The localization of interest was the nucleus, where 366 of the 861 training examples resided.

To build a database for analyses, we renormalized the tables to arrive at a target table with one record per example. We decided to keep information about the genes/proteins themselves and those about their interaction partners separate. Interaction partners are also called neighbors, hence the extension _n in the corresponding table names. We kept the separation because of the different relevance of the data to be assumed for the learning problem and because gene/protein information should not be obscured by the overwhelming amount of such information about their neighbors.

With respect to interactions, we included only those of a certain strength. Furthermore, we made symmetry explicit. That means, we introduced an entry for a relationship between genes/proteins B and A, if there was an interaction between A and B in the original data. We also exploited assumptions on transitivity of the interaction relation, up to a certain number of steps from one gene/protein to the other. Systems such as PROGOL could have used rules for issues such as symmetry. However, producing explicit entries in the interaction table was useful for deciding about when to stop this potentially explosive process.

Test examples were included in the considerations via their interactions with training examples. The resulting schema of our database can be seen in Fig. B.10.

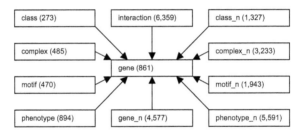

Figure B.10: The KDD Cup 2001 gene data set: database in a new star schema (arrows represent foreign key relationships)

This database was produced directly from the original data set or rather their import into MySQL tables. It is already in a new star schema. This database was the starting point for the application of all learning systems used in our experiments.

A minor issue to note is that many attributes contain rather unusual nominal values here, especially w. r. t. their length. Also, special characters can be found here that caused difficulties for the usage of the data not only when it came to their import into MySQL tables, but also with some learning systems like FOIL. Commas within strings — even when strings were enclosed by apostrophes — caused FOIL to fault. Moreover, original data values such as "?" or "Unknown" had to be replaced by NULL values in the database.

Another minor point was that contrary to the intention of task 3, there were two localizations provided for one of the genes/proteins in the training set. We removed this example from our analyses.

These issues again point to the necessity of human intervention during preprocessing and the opportunity to combine these interventions with the construction of a database in a new star schema.

B.7   Further Data Sets

We investigated several other data sets w.r.t. applicability of RELAGGS and usability for experiments reported on in this dissertation. In this section, we give an overview in order to provide pointers to those data sets and learning tasks for the interested reader. We also explain why certain tasks were *not* considered for our experiments here.

For the KDD Cup 2002 task 2, another data set was provided describing yeast genes [25]. It can be found in the internet at

```
http://www.biostat.wisc.edu/~craven/kddcup/
```

We were able to use similar preparations of the data here as those reported for the KDD Cup 2001 data above. We reached comparatively good results [64, 68, 69, 70]. However, the distribution of the class attribute was very skewed here, hence the application of ROC analyses. Since we chose to present overall accuracy or error rates, respectively, for our experiments in a unified way, we made no use of this learning task here.

Nevertheless, we would like to hint at special aspects of data preparation, viz. the enrichment of the tables by values extracted from abstracts of contributions in the domain of yeast gene research. We were motivated to try those extractions by the many missing values in the original data. It turned out that simple methods for information extraction following ideas from the literature [24, 80, 100] were effective w.r.t. improvements of the ROC areas.

For the KDD Cup 2003, analyses in the domain of publications of physics research literature was chosen. Data and tasks can be found on the web:

```
http://www.cs.cornell.edu/projects/kddcup/
```

For task 1, we again applied RELAGGS to enable a type of time-series analyses rather successfully, reaching the fourth best result (personal communication with Johannes Gehrke by e-mail on Aug-21-2003). However, this kind of experiment was rather different from those reported in this thesis.

For the PKDD Challenges from 1999 to 2001, a medical data set [138] was issued beside the financial one that we dealt with above. We also worked with those data [72, 73] and observed interesting circumstances. We chose as a learning task to predict the occurrence of a certain disease. The first results of the application of RELAGGS achieved very high accuracies.

However, an inspection of the model, a decision tree, showed that it was not applicable for prediction. In its root node it asked for the number of visits of a patient. It positively predicted the patient to have the disease in question, if it was his or her first visit to the hospital. Clearly, the number of visits was one of the aggregate function values computed by RELAGGS.

The good performance of this model was caused by the fact that the hospital had specialized in the diagnosis and treatment of the disease in question such that patients were sent here by other physicians who had developed the corresponding suspicion. Obviously, this points to traps that can be connected to the blind usage of data mining results and shows the usefulness of comprehensible models.

Applying support vector machines, we would probably not have detected this issue. This is also one of the reasons for using mainly decision trees for our experiments reported in this thesis.

More relational data sets can be found on the web, e. g. at or via

```
http://kdd.ics.uci.edu/
http://www-ai.ijs.si/~ilpnet2/apps/index.html
http://www.mlnet.org/
```

We also investigated a number of propositional data sets, among them from the CoIL 2000 Challenge [63], from the Data Mining Cups [66], from the SAS Mining Challenges [115, 65, 42, 43, 44], and other KDD Cups than those mentioned above [56], and also from the UCI ML archive [11]. Working with those data sets, we usually applied conventional feature construction as opposed to aggregate functions for feature construction as used by RELAGGS.

Often, we could observe the application of aggregate functions for the construction of the data sets provided for the competitions, since attributes were usually described in sufficient detail. However, it was in general difficult, if not impossible, to rebuild the original relational databases in order to use them in the scheme of our experiments described in this dissertation. More details about the investigations can be found in the diploma thesis by Körnig [57].

Further real-life datasets were investigated in a number of student research projects. These data are mostly from German car manufacturers, but the original data sets had to remain at their owners for reasons of their relevance for the companies. That is why we could not make favorable use of them for our experiments here. We can only mention some preliminary results.

Following the student research project by Gerdelbracht [35], he also investigated opportunities to apply RELAGGS to predict damages in cars, especially based on the special equipment of the cars. For example learning tasks concerning 20,000 cases of damages for a special type of cars, RELAGGS and WEKA's J48 were able arrive at trees with a few thousand nodes, in a few hours, to improve error rates significantly compared to default error rates. However, the economic relevance of the models learned has not yet been evaluated.

In the diploma thesis by Flach [33], there is an example of a real-life data set analysis in the domain of logistics. The basis for the investigations is a relational database for the management of transport capacities. Troublesome cases of transport should be described by KDD models.

The database is essentially in a star schema as known from data warehouses, such that non-target tables can be joined to the target relation directly, without the application of aggregate functions or other means of propositionalization. Exactly those joins would also be performed by RELAGGS in this situation. Learning results showed slight improvements over default error rates.

Appendix C

Example Scripts and Log Files

In this appendix, we provide further details about the process of the creation of a MySQL database from the original text file data and its transformation into a new star. We chose the Loan.status prediction learning task data as an illustrative example.

C.1 From Text Files to a MySQL Database

The data are provided as text files in the style of the following excerpt, taken from the loan.asc file.

```
"loan_id";"account_id";"date";"amount";"duration";"payments";"status"
5314;1787;930705;96396;12;8033.00;"B"
5316;1801;930711;165960;36;4610.00;"A"
6863;9188;930728;127080;60;2118.00;"A"
5325;1843;930803;105804;36;2939.00;"A"
7240;11013;930906;274740;60;4579.00;"A"
6687;8261;930913;87840;24;3660.00;"A"
7284;11265;930915;52788;12;4399.00;"A"
6111;5428;930924;174744;24;7281.00;"B"
7235;10973;931013;154416;48;3217.00;"A"
5997;4894;931104;117024;24;4876.00;"A"
```

The following statements were used to create a relational database. Tables are created and filled from the original text file data. Statements for one table are grouped and separated from others by double empty lines. Note the speed of the process: the import of more than one million records for transactions takes only 42.3 sec, for example.

We further point the interested reader to some special treatment of the data, e. g. replacing empty strings with more appropriate NULL values in table **trans**. For some other tables, similar editing was executed for the original text files. These and other minor preparation steps, which led from the **asc** files as provided by the organizers of the Challenge to the **txt** files as used here, are described in a separate report that is available on request.

```
create database test_pkdd_1999_finance_original;

use test_pkdd_1999_finance_original;


create table loan (
loan_id integer not null,
account_id integer not null,
date integer,
amount integer,
duration integer,
payments integer,
status char,
primary key (loan_id));

desc loan;

load data local infile 'loan.txt' into table loan
fields terminated by ';' optionally enclosed by '"'
lines terminated by '\r\n' ignore 1 lines;

select * from loan limit 10;

select count(distinct status) from loan;

select status, count(*) from loan group by status;


create table account (
account_id integer not null,
district_id integer not null,
frequency varchar(32),
date integer,
primary key (account_id));

desc account;

load data local infile 'account.txt' into table account
fields terminated by ';' optionally enclosed by '"'
lines terminated by '\r\n' ignore 1 lines;


create table order_ (
order_id integer not null,
account_id integer not null,
bank_to char(2),
account_to varchar(32),
amount double,
k_symbol varchar(32),
primary key (order_id));

desc order_;

load data local infile 'order.txt' into table order_
fields terminated by ';' optionally enclosed by '"'
lines terminated by '\r\n' ignore 1 lines;


create table trans (
trans_id integer not null,
account_id integer not null,
date integer,
type varchar(32),
operation varchar(32),
```

```
amount double,
balance double,
k_symbol varchar(32),
bank char(2),
account varchar(32),
primary key (trans_id));

desc trans;

load data local infile 'trans.txt' into table trans
fields terminated by ';' optionally enclosed by '"'
lines terminated by '\r\n' ignore 1 lines;

update trans set k_symbol = NULL where k_symbol = "";

update trans set account = NULL where account = "";


create table disp (
disp_id integer not null,
client_id integer not null,
account_id integer not null,
type varchar(32),
primary key (disp_id));

desc disp;

load data local infile 'disp.txt' into table disp
fields terminated by ';' optionally enclosed by '"'
lines terminated by '\r\n' ignore 1 lines;


create table card (
card_id integer not null,
disp_id integer not null,
type varchar(32),
issued integer,
primary key (card_id));

desc card;

load data local infile 'card.txt' into table card
fields terminated by ';' optionally enclosed by '"'
lines terminated by '\r\n' ignore 1 lines;


create table client (
client_id integer not null,
birth_number integer,
district_id integer not null,
primary key (client_id));

desc client;

load data local infile 'client.txt' into table client
fields terminated by ';' optionally enclosed by '"'
lines terminated by '\r\n' ignore 1 lines;


create table district (
A1 integer not null,
A2 varchar(32),
A3 varchar(32),
A4 integer,
A5 integer,
```

```
A6 integer,
A7 integer,
A8 integer,
A9 integer,
A10 double,
A11 integer,
A12 double,
A13 double,
A14 integer,
A15 integer,
A16 integer,
primary key (A1));

desc district;

load data local infile 'district.txt' into table district
fields terminated by ';' optionally enclosed by '"'
lines terminated by '\r\n' ignore 1 lines;


show tables;
```

The log file that was produced by MySQL with the `tee` command for running the statements shown above follows. Unfortunately, the statements are not repeated by `tee`. However, the reader may simply find the relationships to `desc` statements from the script above, focusing on the primary key attribute names (Key − PRI) in table descriptions, for an orientation.

```
mysql> source ALL.sql
Query OK, 1 row affected (0.13 sec)

Database changed
Query OK, 0 rows affected (0.15 sec)

+------------+----------+------+-----+---------+-------+
| Field      | Type     | Null | Key | Default | Extra |
+------------+----------+------+-----+---------+-------+
| loan_id    | int(11)  |      | PRI | 0       |       |
| account_id | int(11)  |      |     | 0       |       |
| date       | int(11)  | YES  |     | NULL    |       |
| amount     | int(11)  | YES  |     | NULL    |       |
| duration   | int(11)  | YES  |     | NULL    |       |
| payments   | int(11)  | YES  |     | NULL    |       |
| status     | char(1)  | YES  |     | NULL    |       |
+------------+----------+------+-----+---------+-------+
7 rows in set (0.03 sec)

Query OK, 682 rows affected (0.16 sec)
Records: 682  Deleted: 0  Skipped: 0  Warnings: 0

+---------+------------+--------+--------+----------+----------+--------+
| loan_id | account_id | date   | amount | duration | payments | status |
+---------+------------+--------+--------+----------+----------+--------+
|    5314 |       1787 | 930705 |  96396 |       12 |     8033 | B      |
|    5316 |       1801 | 930711 | 165960 |       36 |     4610 | A      |
|    6863 |       9188 | 930728 | 127080 |       60 |     2118 | A      |
|    5325 |       1843 | 930803 | 105804 |       36 |     2939 | A      |
|    7240 |      11013 | 930906 | 274740 |       60 |     4579 | A      |
|    6687 |       8261 | 930913 |  87840 |       24 |     3660 | A      |
|    7284 |      11265 | 930915 |  52788 |       12 |     4399 | A      |
```

```
|    6111 |        5428 | 930924 | 174744 |         24 |    7281 | B    |
|    7235 |       10973 | 931013 | 154416 |         48 |    3217 | A    |
|    5997 |        4894 | 931104 | 117024 |         24 |    4876 | A    |
+---------+------------+--------+--------+----------+---------+-------+
10 rows in set (0.04 sec)

+------------------------+
| count(distinct status) |
+------------------------+
|                      4 |
+------------------------+
1 row in set (0.03 sec)

+--------+----------+
| status | count(*) |
+--------+----------+
| A      |      203 |
| B      |       31 |
| C      |      403 |
| D      |       45 |
+--------+----------+
4 rows in set (0.01 sec)

Query OK, 0 rows affected (0.05 sec)

+-------------+-------------+------+-----+---------+-------+
| Field       | Type        | Null | Key | Default | Extra |
+-------------+-------------+------+-----+---------+-------+
| account_id  | int(11)     |      | PRI | 0       |       |
| district_id | int(11)     |      |     | 0       |       |
| frequency   | varchar(32) | YES  |     | NULL    |       |
| date        | int(11)     | YES  |     | NULL    |       |
+-------------+-------------+------+-----+---------+-------+
4 rows in set (0.00 sec)

Query OK, 4500 rows affected (0.16 sec)
Records: 4500  Deleted: 0  Skipped: 0  Warnings: 0

Query OK, 0 rows affected (0.05 sec)

+-------------+-------------+------+-----+---------+-------+
| Field       | Type        | Null | Key | Default | Extra |
+-------------+-------------+------+-----+---------+-------+
| order_id    | int(11)     |      | PRI | 0       |       |
| account_id  | int(11)     |      |     | 0       |       |
| bank_to     | char(2)     | YES  |     | NULL    |       |
| account_to  | varchar(32) | YES  |     | NULL    |       |
| amount      | double      | YES  |     | NULL    |       |
| k_symbol    | varchar(32) | YES  |     | NULL    |       |
+-------------+-------------+------+-----+---------+-------+
6 rows in set (0.00 sec)

Query OK, 6471 rows affected (0.30 sec)
Records: 6471  Deleted: 0  Skipped: 0  Warnings: 0

Query OK, 0 rows affected (0.06 sec)

+-------------+-------------+------+-----+---------+-------+
| Field       | Type        | Null | Key | Default | Extra |
+-------------+-------------+------+-----+---------+-------+
| trans_id    | int(11)     |      | PRI | 0       |       |
| account_id  | int(11)     |      |     | 0       |       |
| date        | int(11)     | YES  |     | NULL    |       |
| type        | varchar(32) | YES  |     | NULL    |       |
| operation   | varchar(32) | YES  |     | NULL    |       |
```

```
| amount    | double      | YES |     | NULL    |       |
| balance   | double      | YES |     | NULL    |       |
| k_symbol  | varchar(32) | YES |     | NULL    |       |
| bank      | char(2)     | YES |     | NULL    |       |
| account   | varchar(32) | YES |     | NULL    |       |
+-----------+-------------+-----+-----+---------+-------+
10 rows in set (0.01 sec)

Query OK, 1056320 rows affected (41.26 sec)
Records: 1056320  Deleted: 0  Skipped: 0  Warnings: 0

Query OK, 53433 rows affected (21.52 sec)
Rows matched: 53433  Changed: 53433  Warnings: 0

Query OK, 10 rows affected (17.96 sec)
Rows matched: 10  Changed: 10  Warnings: 0

Query OK, 0 rows affected (0.05 sec)

+------------+-------------+------+-----+---------+-------+
| Field      | Type        | Null | Key | Default | Extra |
+------------+-------------+------+-----+---------+-------+
| disp_id    | int(11)     |      | PRI | 0       |       |
| client_id  | int(11)     |      |     | 0       |       |
| account_id | int(11)     |      |     | 0       |       |
| type       | varchar(32) | YES  |     | NULL    |       |
+------------+-------------+------+-----+---------+-------+
4 rows in set (0.00 sec)

Query OK, 5369 rows affected (0.09 sec)
Records: 5369  Deleted: 0  Skipped: 0  Warnings: 0

Query OK, 0 rows affected (0.05 sec)

+---------+-------------+------+-----+---------+-------+
| Field   | Type        | Null | Key | Default | Extra |
+---------+-------------+------+-----+---------+-------+
| card_id | int(11)     |      | PRI | 0       |       |
| disp_id | int(11)     |      |     | 0       |       |
| type    | varchar(32) | YES  |     | NULL    |       |
| issued  | int(11)     | YES  |     | NULL    |       |
+---------+-------------+------+-----+---------+-------+
4 rows in set (0.00 sec)

Query OK, 892 rows affected (0.02 sec)
Records: 892  Deleted: 0  Skipped: 0  Warnings: 0

Query OK, 0 rows affected (0.05 sec)

+--------------+---------+------+-----+---------+-------+
| Field        | Type    | Null | Key | Default | Extra |
+--------------+---------+------+-----+---------+-------+
| client_id    | int(11) |      | PRI | 0       |       |
| birth_number | int(11) | YES  |     | NULL    |       |
| district_id  | int(11) |      |     | 0       |       |
+--------------+---------+------+-----+---------+-------+
3 rows in set (0.00 sec)

Query OK, 5369 rows affected (0.05 sec)
Records: 5369  Deleted: 0  Skipped: 0  Warnings: 0

Query OK, 0 rows affected (0.06 sec)

+-------+-------------+------+-----+---------+-------+
| Field | Type        | Null | Key | Default | Extra |
```

```
+-------+-------------+------+-----+---------+-------+
| A1    | int(11)     |      | PRI | 0       |       |
| A2    | varchar(32) | YES  |     | NULL    |       |
| A3    | varchar(32) | YES  |     | NULL    |       |
| A4    | int(11)     | YES  |     | NULL    |       |
| A5    | int(11)     | YES  |     | NULL    |       |
| A6    | int(11)     | YES  |     | NULL    |       |
| A7    | int(11)     | YES  |     | NULL    |       |
| A8    | int(11)     | YES  |     | NULL    |       |
| A9    | int(11)     | YES  |     | NULL    |       |
| A10   | double      | YES  |     | NULL    |       |
| A11   | int(11)     | YES  |     | NULL    |       |
| A12   | double      | YES  |     | NULL    |       |
| A13   | double      | YES  |     | NULL    |       |
| A14   | int(11)     | YES  |     | NULL    |       |
| A15   | int(11)     | YES  |     | NULL    |       |
| A16   | int(11)     | YES  |     | NULL    |       |
+-------+-------------+------+-----+---------+-------+
16 rows in set (0.00 sec)

Query OK, 77 rows affected (0.01 sec)
Records: 77  Deleted: 0  Skipped: 0  Warnings: 0

+-------------------------------------------+
| Tables_in_test_pkdd_1999_finance_original |
+-------------------------------------------+
| account                                   |
| card                                      |
| client                                    |
| disp                                      |
| district                                  |
| loan                                      |
| order_                                    |
| trans                                     |
+-------------------------------------------+
8 rows in set (0.00 sec)

mysql> exit
```

C.2   New Star Generation

The following statements were used to produce a database in a new star schema
for Loan.status prediction, from the database described in the preceding section.
For each table, there is an **explain** statement to indicate prospective performance of the **select** statement, which is afterwards used in the **create table**
statement. Index creation is also listed. Statements for one table are grouped
and separated from others by double empty lines. Note special treatments for
table **trans** with the date restrictions, and of table **client** with an attribute
split.

```
create database test_pkdd_1999_finance_new_star;

use test_pkdd_1999_finance_new_star;

explain
```

```
select *
from test_pkdd_1999_finance_original.loan;

create table loan (primary key (loan_id))
select *
from test_pkdd_1999_finance_original.loan;

create index account_id on loan (account_id);


explain
select l.loan_id, a.*
from loan l,
     test_pkdd_1999_finance_original.account a
where l.account_id = a.account_id;

create table account (primary key (loan_id))
select l.loan_id, a.*
from loan l,
     test_pkdd_1999_finance_original.account a
where l.account_id = a.account_id;


explain
select l.loan_id, o.*
from loan l,
     test_pkdd_1999_finance_original.order_ o
where l.account_id = o.account_id;

create table order  (key (loan id))
select l.loan_id, o.*
from loan l,
     test_pkdd_1999_finance_original.order_ o
where l.account_id = o.account_id;


explain
select l.loan_id, t.*
from loan l,
     test_pkdd_1999_finance_original.trans t
where l.account_id = t.account_id and
      l.date > t.date;

create table trans (key (loan_id))
select l.loan_id, t.*
from loan l,
     test_pkdd_1999_finance_original.trans t
where l.account_id = t.account_id and
      l.date > t.date;


explain
select l.loan_id, d.*
from loan l,
     test_pkdd_1999_finance_original.disp d
where l.account_id = d.account_id;

create table disp (key (loan_id))
select l.loan_id, d.*
from loan l,
     test_pkdd_1999_finance_original.disp d
where l.account_id = d.account_id;


explain
```

```
select l.loan_id, c.*
from loan l,
     disp d,
     test_pkdd_1999_finance_original.card c
where l.account_id = d.account_id and
      d.disp_id = c.disp_id and
      l.date > c.issued;

create table card (key (loan_id))
select l.loan_id, c.*
from loan l,
     disp d,
     test_pkdd_1999_finance_original.card c
where l.account_id = d.account_id and
      d.disp_id = c.disp_id and
      l.date > c.issued;


explain
select d.loan_id, c.*
from disp d,
     test_pkdd_1999_finance_original.client c
where d.client_id = c.client_id;

create table client (key (loan_id))
select d.loan_id, c.*
from disp d,
     test_pkdd_1999_finance_original.client c
where d.client_id = c.client_id;

alter table client add column (gender char);

update client set gender = 'm'
where birth_number % 10000 < 1300;

update client set gender = 'f', birth_number = birth_number - 5000
where birth_number % 10000 > 1300;

alter table client change birth_number birthday integer;


explain
select a.loan_id, d.*
from account a,
     test_pkdd_1999_finance_original.district d
where a.district_id = d.a1
union all
select c.loan_id, d.*
from client c,
     test_pkdd_1999_finance_original.district d
where c.district_id = d.a1;

create table district (key (loan_id))
select a.loan_id, d.*
from account a,
     test_pkdd_1999_finance_original.district d
where a.district_id = d.a1
union all
select c.loan_id, d.*
from client c,
     test_pkdd_1999_finance_original.district d
where c.district_id = d.a1;


show tables;
```

Here is the log file that was produced by MySQL for running the statements shown above. Short names of tables in the results of **explain** statements may enable a reference to those **explain** statements in the script above, for an orientation.

```
mysql> source ALL_SQL.txt
Query OK, 1 row affected (0.04 sec)

Database changed
+-------+------+---------------+------+---------+------+------+-------+
| table | type | possible_keys | key  | key_len | ref  | rows | Extra |
+-------+------+---------------+------+---------+------+------+-------+
| loan  | ALL  | NULL          | NULL |    NULL | NULL |  682 |       |
+-------+------+---------------+------+---------+------+------+-------+
1 row in set (0.00 sec)

Query OK, 682 rows affected (0.07 sec)
Records: 682  Duplicates: 0  Warnings: 0

Query OK, 682 rows affected (0.22 sec)
Records: 682  Duplicates: 0  Warnings: 0

+-------+--------+---------------+---------+---------+--------------+------+-------+
| table | type   | possible_keys | key     | key_len | ref          | rows | Extra |
+-------+--------+---------------+---------+---------+--------------+------+-------+
| l     | ALL    | account_id    | NULL    |    NULL | NULL         |  682 |       |
| a     | eq_ref | PRIMARY       | PRIMARY |       4 | l.account_id |    1 |       |
+-------+--------+---------------+---------+---------+--------------+------+-------+
2 rows in set (0.01 sec)

Query OK, 682 rows affected (0.10 sec)
Records: 682  Duplicates: 0  Warnings: 0

+-------+------+---------------+------------+---------+--------------+------+-------+
| table | type | possible_keys | key        | key_len | ref          | rows | Extra |
+-------+------+---------------+------------+---------+--------------+------+-------+
| o     | ALL  | NULL          | NULL       |    NULL | NULL         | 6471 |       |
| l     | ref  | account_id    | account_id |       4 | o.account_id |    1 |       |
+-------+------+---------------+------------+---------+--------------+------+-------+
2 rows in set (0.00 sec)

Query OK, 1513 rows affected (0.22 sec)
Records: 1513  Duplicates: 0  Warnings: 0

+-------+------+---------------+------------+---------+--------------+---------+-------------+
| table | type | possible_keys | key        | key_len | ref          | rows    | Extra       |
+-------+------+---------------+------------+---------+--------------+---------+-------------+
| t     | ALL  | NULL          | NULL       |    NULL | NULL         | 1056320 |             |
| l     | ref  | account_id    | account_id |       4 | t.account_id |       1 | Using where |
+-------+------+---------------+------------+---------+--------------+---------+-------------+
2 rows in set (0.00 sec)

Query OK, 54694 rows affected (12.84 sec)
Records: 54694  Duplicates: 0  Warnings: 0

+-------+------+---------------+------+---------+------+------+-------+
| table | type | possible_keys | key  | key_len | ref  | rows | Extra |
+-------+------+---------------+------+---------+------+------+-------+
| d     | ALL  | NULL          | NULL |    NULL | NULL | 5369 |       |
```

```
| 1    | ref  | account_id    | account_id |      4 | d.account_id |   1 |      |
+------+------+---------------+------------+--------+--------------+------+------+
2 rows in set (0.00 sec)

Query OK, 827 rows affected (0.12 sec)
Records: 827  Duplicates: 0  Warnings: 0
```

```
+-------+------+---------------+------------+---------+--------------+------+-------------+
| table | type | possible_keys | key        | key_len | ref          | rows | Extra       |
+-------+------+---------------+------------+---------+--------------+------+-------------+
| d     | ALL  | NULL          | NULL       | NULL    | NULL         | 827  |             |
| 1     | ref  | account_id    | account_id |       4 | d.account_id |   1  |             |
| c     | ALL  | NULL          | NULL       | NULL    | NULL         | 892  | Using where |
+-------+------+---------------+------------+---------+--------------+------+-------------+
3 rows in set (0.00 sec)

Query OK, 36 rows affected (0.61 sec)
Records: 36  Duplicates: 0  Warnings: 0
```

```
+-------+--------+---------------+---------+---------+-------------+------+-------+
| table | type   | possible_keys | key     | key_len | ref         | rows | Extra |
+-------+--------+---------------+---------+---------+-------------+------+-------+
| d     | ALL    | NULL          | NULL    | NULL    | NULL        | 827  |       |
| c     | eq_ref | PRIMARY       | PRIMARY |       4 | d.client_id |   1  |       |
+-------+--------+---------------+---------+---------+-------------+------+-------+
2 rows in set (0.00 sec)

Query OK, 827 rows affected (0.06 sec)
Records: 827  Duplicates: 0  Warnings: 0

Query OK, 827 rows affected (0.21 sec)
Records: 827  Duplicates: 0  Warnings: 0

Query OK, 410 rows affected (0.00 sec)
Rows matched: 410  Changed: 410  Warnings: 0

Query OK, 417 rows affected (0.01 sec)
Rows matched: 417  Changed: 417  Warnings: 0

Query OK, 827 rows affected (0.18 sec)
Records: 827  Duplicates: 0  Warnings: 0
```

```
+-------+--------+---------------+---------+---------+---------------+------+-------+
| table | type   | possible_keys | key     | key_len | ref           | rows | Extra |
+-------+--------+---------------+---------+---------+---------------+------+-------+
| a     | ALL    | NULL          | NULL    | NULL    | NULL          | 682  |       |
| d     | eq_ref | PRIMARY       | PRIMARY |       4 | a.district_id |   1  |       |
| c     | ALL    | NULL          | NULL    | NULL    | NULL          | 827  |       |
| d     | eq_ref | PRIMARY       | PRIMARY |       4 | c.district_id |   1  |       |
+-------+--------+---------------+---------+---------+---------------+------+-------+
4 rows in set (0.03 sec)

Query OK, 1509 rows affected (0.15 sec)
Records: 1509  Duplicates: 0  Warnings: 0
```

```
+------------------------------------------+
| Tables_in_test_pkdd_1999_finance_new_star |
+------------------------------------------+
| account                                  |
| card                                     |
| client                                   |
| disp                                     |
| district                                 |
| loan                                     |
| order_                                   |
```

```
| trans                                       |
+---------------------------------------------+
8 rows in set (0.01 sec)

mysql> exit
```

Direct propagation of *loan_id* to tables *trans* and *card* is a deviation from the general procedure for new star generation. Here, it was preferred as a simple opportunity for the exclusion of transactions and cards dating after loan grantings, cf. Appendix B.

Scripts and log files such as those listed above as well as other material from our experiments are available from the author on request.

Appendix D

Running Example

For the illustration of many facets of relational learning, we introduce an example database in this appendix. However, we also use other, especially tailored examples in certain cases, in order not to overcomplicate our running example database.

Figure D.1 shows the relational database for our running example. We adopt to the case that all tables have a primary key consisting of a single integer attribute. This corresponds to rules for efficient database design.

Even if such an attribute is not available in an original table, it can be easily constructed by enumerating its rows. The basic assumption here is that within one table, different rows describe different objects. If this is not the case, normalization can remedy the situation.

The schema contains several relevant situations that often occur in real-life databases.

For instance, there are one-to-many relationships, e. g. between elements in tables T and A, similarly those in T and B.

There are also many-to-many relationships, e. g. between elements in T and E via D.

Furthermore, we included examples of reachability of relations via several paths in the induced undirected graph, e. g. E can be reached from T via D and via F.

The running example is not intended to illustrate issues such as the usage of views or rules as part of the database. Neither does it contain any data that are meant to show any meaning beyond the demonstration of the existence of numeric and nominal types.

We are aware of the circumstance that examples with meaningful data can be easier to read. However, we think that the example data favorably demonstrate the largely semantics-blind perspective of data mining systems and also of our variant of propositionalization.

Of course, in real-life data mining projects, an evaluation of the learning results should include a check of plausibility by domain experts. Such investigations were accomplished as far as possible in our empirical work, but are not in the focus of the usage of our running example.

The relations from the database can be written down as Prolog clauses, e. g. in the following way:

```
t(1,1,1,pos).
t(2,2,2,neg).
...
a(1,1,1,10,x).
...
f(1,1,1,1000,?).
f(2,1,1,,2000,?).
...
```

Type information for the arguments of the predicates is not explicitely given here, but may be provided with the help of extra predicates as usual in mode declarations used for many up-to-date ILP systems.

Further, the question mark constant is used in many ILP systems to denote missing values or NULL values as known from relational databases.

Predicate symbols start with a small letter, by Prolog conventions. Table names begin with a capital letter. Table names should not be confused with variable names in Prolog statements or other symbols used in the text. Context information is supposed to avoid misunderstandings.

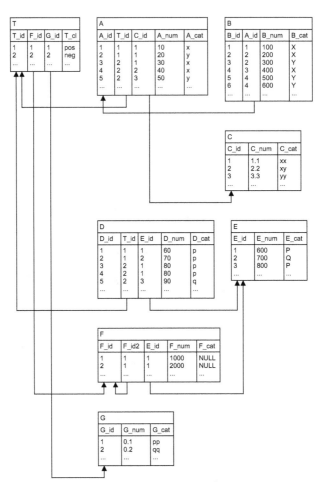

Figure D.1: A running example database schema and contents (8 tables are depicted by the rectangles with table names in the first lines, attribute names in the second lines, and attribute values below; arrows represent foreign key relationships, conventionally drawn from foreign key attributes to primary key attributes)

Bibliography

[1] Serge Abiteboul, Richard Hull, and Victor Vianu. *Foundations of Databases*. Addison-Wesley Publishing, 1995.

[2] Rakesh Agrawal, Tomasz Imielinski, and Arun N. Swami. Mining association rules between sets of items in large databases. In Peter Buneman and Sushil Jajodia, editors, *Proceedings of the ACM SIGMOD International Conference on Management of Data*, pages 207–216. ACM Press, 1993.

[3] Érick Alphonse and Stan Matwin. Feature Subset Selection and Inductive Logic Programming. In Clause Sammut and Achim G. Hoffmann, editors, *Proceedings of the Nineteenth International Conference on Machine Learning (ICML)*, pages 11–18. Morgan Kaufmann, 2002.

[4] Érick Alphonse and Céline Rouveirol. Lazy propositionalisation for Relational Learning. In Werner Horn, editor, *Proceedings of the Fourteenth European Conference on Artificial Intelligence (ECAI)*, pages 256–260. IOS Press, 2000.

[5] Anna Atramentov, Hector Leiva, and Vasant Honavar. A Multi-relational Decision Tree Learning Algorithm – Implementation and Experiments. In Tamás Horváth and Akihiro Yamamoto, editors, *Proceedings of the Thirteenth International Conference on Inductive Logic Programming (ILP)*, LNAI 2835, pages 38–56. Springer-Verlag, 2003.

[6] Andreas Bauer and Holger Günzel. *Data-Warehouse-Systeme: Architektur, Entwicklung, Anwendung*. dpunkt.verlag, 2001.

[7] Siegfried Bell and Peter Brockhausen. Discovery of Constraints and Data Dependencies in Databases (Extended Abstract). In Nada Lavrač and Stefan Wrobel, editors, *Proceedings of the Eighth European Conference on Machine Learning (ECML)*, LNCS 912, pages 267–270. Springer-Verlag, 1995.

[8] Petr Berka. Guide to the Financial Data Set. In Arno Siebes and Petr Berka, editors, *PKDD2000 Discovery Challenge*, 2000.

[9] Petr Berka, Marta Sochorová, and Jan Rauch. Sisyphus data analysis using GUHA and KEX. In *KDD Sisyphus Challenge*, 1998.

[10] Michael J. A. Berry and Gordon S. Linoff. *Mastering Data Mining.* Wiley, 2000.

[11] C. L. Blake and Christopher John Merz. *UCI Repository of machine learning databases: http://www.ics.uci.edu/~mlearn/MLRepository.html.* University of California, Irvine, Dept. of Information and Computer Sciences, 1998.

[12] Jan Blaťák and Luboš Popelínský. Feature Construction with RAP. In Tamás Horváth and Akihiro Yamamoto, editors, *Proceedings of the Work-in-progress track of the Thirteenth International Conference on Inductive Logic Programming (ILP)*, pages 1–11, 2003.

[13] Hendrik Blockeel and Maurice Bruynooghe. Aggregation vs. selection bias, and relational neural networks. In David Jensen and Lise Getoor, editors, *Proceedings of the IJCAI-2003 Workshop on Learning Statistical Models from Relational Data (SRL)*, 2003.

[14] Hendrik Blockeel and Luc De Raedt. Top-Down Induction of First-Order Logical Decision Trees. *Artificial Intelligence*, 101(1-2):285–297, 1998.

[15] Christian Borgelt. *Data Mining with Graphical Models.* PhD thesis, Otto-von-Guericke-Universität, Fakultät für Informatik, Institut für Wissens- und Sprachverarbeitung, 2000.

[16] Christian Borgelt, Frank Klawonn, Rudolf Kruse, and Detlef Nauck. *Neuro-Fuzzy-Systeme.* Vieweg, 3rd edition, 2003.

[17] Isabelle Bournaud, Mélanie Courtine, and Jean-Daniel Zucker. Proposition-alization for Clustering Symbolic Relational Descriptions. In Stan Matwin and Claude Sammut, editors, *Proceedings of the Twelfth International Conference on Inductive Logic Programming (ILP)*, LNAI 2538, pages 1–16. Springer-Verlag, 2002.

[18] Ivan Bratko, Igor Mozetič, and Nada Lavrač. *KARDIO: A Study in Deep and Qualitative Knowledge for Expert Systems.* MIT Press, 1989.

[19] Leo Breiman, Jerome H. Friedman, Richard A. Olshen, and Charles J. Stone. *Classification and Regression Trees.* Wadsworth, 1984.

[20] Christopher J. C. Burges. A Tutorial on Support Vector Machines for Pattern Recognition. *Data Mining and Knowledge Discovery*, 2(2):121–167, 1998.

[21] Luca Cabibbo and Riccardo Torlone. A Framework for the Investigation of Aggregate Functions in Database Queries. In Catriel Beeri and Peter

Bruneman, editors, *Proceedings of the Seventh International Conference on Database Theory (ICDT)*, LNCS 1540, pages 383–397. Springer-Verlag, 1999.

[22] Jie Cheng, Christos Hatzis, Hisashi Hayashi, Mark-A. Krogel, Shinichi Morishita, David Page, and Jun Sese. KDD Cup 2001 Report. *SIGKDD Explorations*, 3(2):47–64, 2002.

[23] William F. Clocksin and Christopher S. Mellish. *Programming in Prolog: Using the ISO Standard*. Springer-Verlag, 2003.

[24] William W. Cohen. Automatically Extracting Features for Concept Learning from the Web. In Pat Langley, editor, *Proceedings of the Seventeenth International Conference on Machine Learning (ICML)*, pages 159–166. Morgan Kaufmann, 2000.

[25] Mark Craven. The Genomics of a Signaling Pathway: A KDD Cup Challenge Task. *SIGKDD Explorations*, 4(2):97–98, 2002.

[26] Jürgen Dassow. *Logik für Informatiker*. B. G. Teubner, 2005.

[27] Luc Dehaspe and Luc De Raedt. Mining Association Rules in Multiple Relations. In Nada Lavrač and Sašo Džeroski, editors, *Proceedings of the Seventh International Workshop on Inductive Logic Programming (ILP)*, LNAI 1297, pages 125–132. Springer-Verlag, 1997.

[28] Luc Dehaspe and Hannu Toivonen. Discovery of Relational Association Rules. In Nada Lavrač and Sašo Džeroski, editors, *Relational Data Mining*. Springer-Verlag, 2001.

[29] Marcin Detyniecki. *Mathematical aggregation operators and their application to video querying*. PhD thesis, Laboratoire d'Informatique de Paris 6, France, 2000.

[30] Timm Euler, Detlef Geppert, Olaf Rem, and Martin Scholz. *The Mining-Mart User Guide*. Universität Dortmund, 2004.

[31] Ludwig Fahrmeir, Rita Künstler, Iris Pigeot, and Gerhard Tutz. *Statistik: Der Weg zur Datenanalyse*. Springer-Verlag, 3rd edition, 2001.

[32] Usama M. Fayyad, Gregory Piatetsky-Shapiro, and Padhraic Smyth. From Data Mining to Knowledge Discovery: An Overview. In Usama M. Fayyad, Gregory Piatetsky-Shapiro, Padhraic Smyth, and Ramasamy Uthurusamy, editors, *Advances in Knowledge Discovery and Data Mining*. AAAI/MIT Press, 1996.

[33] Aicke Flach. Vergleich von Verfahren zur Klassifikation von multirelational gespeicherten Daten. Diplomarbeit, Otto-von-Guericke-Universität Magdeburg, Fakultät für Informatik, Institut für Technische und Betriebliche Informationssysteme, 2005.

[34] Thomas Gärtner, Shaomin Wu, and Peter A. Flach. Data Mining on the Sisyphus Dataset: Evaluation and Integration of Results. In Christophe Giraud-Carrier, Nada Lavrač, and Steve Moyle, editors, *Proceedings of the ECML/PKDD-2001 Workshop on Integrating Aspects of Data Mining, Decision Support and Meta-Learning (IDDM)*, pages 69–80, 2001.

[35] Stefan Gerdelbracht. Variantenanalyse: Untersuchung von Zusammenhängen zwischen Fahrzeugdaten und Ausfällen. Studienarbeit, Otto-von-Guericke-Universität Magdeburg, Fakultät für Informatik, Institut für Wissens- und Sprachverarbeitung, 2003.

[36] Jim Gray, Surajit Chaudhuri, Adam Bosworth, Andrew Layman, Don Reichart, Murali Venkatrao, Frank Pellow, and Hamid Pirahesh. Data Cube: A Relational Aggregation Operator Generalizing Group-By, Cross-Tab, and Sub-Total. *Data Mining and Knowledge Discovery*, 1(1):29–53, 1997.

[37] Jiawei Han and Micheline Kamber. *Data Mining: Concepts and Techniques*. Morgan Kaufmann, 2000.

[38] David Hand, Heikki Mannila, and Padhraic Smyth. *Principles of Data Mining*. MIT Press, 2001.

[39] John Hertz, Anders Krogh, and Richard G. Palmer. *Introduction to the Theory of Neural Computation*. Addison Wesley, 1991.

[40] Andreas Heuer and Gunter Saake. *Datenbanken — Konzepte und Sprachen*. International Thomson Publishing, 1997.

[41] Andreas Heuer, Gunter Saake, and Kai-Uwe Sattler. *Datenbanken kompakt*. mitp-Verlag, 2001.

[42] Torsten Hildebrandt, Folker Folkens, Mark-A. Krogel, Oliver Priebus, and Jörg Wunderlich. SAS Mining Challenge 2003. *Künstliche Intelligenz*, 18(3):77, 2004.

[43] Torsten Hildebrandt, Folker Folkens, Mark-A. Krogel, Oliver Priebus, and Jörg Wunderlich. SAS Mining Challenge 2003: Abo oder keins? *Datenbank-Spektrum*, 9:59–60, 2004.

[44] Torsten Hildebrandt, Folker Folkens, Mark-A. Krogel, Oliver Priebus, and Jörg Wunderlich. SAS Mining Challenge 2003 Report. In Andreas Bauer, Michael Böhnlein, Olaf Herden, and Wolfgang Lehner, editors, *Proceedings Internationales Symposium: Data-Warehouse-Systeme und Knowledge-Discovery*, pages 65–74. Shaker Verlag, 2004.

[45] Frank Honza. Untersuchung von Data-Mining-Ansätzen für die Analyse von Fahrzeugdaten: Verwaltung von Lastkollektiven und deren Clusterergebnissen. Studienarbeit, Otto-von-Guericke-Universität Magdeburg, Fakultät für Informatik, Institut für Wissens- und Sprachverarbeitung, 2004.

[46] Ykä Huhtala, Juha Kärkkäinen, Pasi Porkka, and Hannu Toivonen. TANE: An Efficient Algorithm for Discovering Functional and Approximate Dependencies. *The Computer Journal*, 42(2):100–111, 1999.

[47] William H. Inmon. *Building the Data Warehose*. Wiley, 3rd edition, 2002.

[48] David Jensen, Jennifer Neville, and Michael Hay. Avoiding Bias when Aggregating Relational Data with Degree Disparity. In Tom Fawcett and Nina Mishra, editors, *Proceedings of the Twentieth International Conference on Machine Learning (ICML)*, pages 274–281. AAAI Press, 2003.

[49] Thorsten Joachims. Making Large-Scale SVM Learning Practical. In Bernhard Schölkopf, Christopher J. C. Burges, and Alexander J. Smola, editors, *Advances in Kernel Methods - Support Vector Learning*. MIT Press, 1999.

[50] Thorsten Joachims. *Learning to Classify Text using Support Vector Machines*. Kluwer Academic Publishers, 2002.

[51] George H. John. *Enhancements to the Data Mining Process*. PhD thesis, Stanford University, Department of Computer Science, CA/USA, 1997.

[52] Jörg-Uwe Kietz, Regina Zücker, and Anca Vaduva. MINING MART: Combining Case-Based Reasoning and Multistrategy Learning into a Framework for Reusing KDD-Applications. In Ryszard S. Michalski and Pavel Brazdil, editors, *Proceedings of the Fifth International Workshop on Multistrategy Learning (MSL)*, 2000.

[53] Arno Knobbe. *Multi-Relational Data Mining*. PhD thesis, Universiteit Utrecht, Faculteit Wiskunde en Informatica; also as SIKS Dissertation Series No. 2004-15, 2004.

[54] Arno J. Knobbe, Marc de Haas, and Arno Siebes. Propositionalisation and Aggregates. In Luc De Raedt and Arno Siebes, editors, *Proceedings of the Fifth European Conference on Principles of Data Mining and Knowledge Disovery (PKDD)*, LNAI 2168, pages 277–288. Springer-Verlag, 2001.

[55] Arno J. Knobbe, Arno Siebes, and Bart Marseille. Involving Aggregate Functions in Multi-relational Search. In Tapio Elomaa, Heikki Mannila, and Hannu Toivonen, editors, *Proceedings of the Sixth European Conference on Principles of Data Mining and Knowledge Disovery (PKDD)*, LNAI 2431, pages 287–298. Springer-Verlag, 2002.

[56] Ron Kohavi, Carla E. Brodley, Brian Frasca, Llew Mason, and Zijan Zheng. KDD-Cup 2000 Organizers' Report: Peeling the Onion. *SIGKDD Explorations*, 2(2):86–98, 2000.

[57] Danny Körnig. Untersuchung zur Verwendung von Aggregatfunktionen für die Wissensentdeckung in Datenbanken. Diplomarbeit, Otto-von-Guericke-Universität Magdeburg, Fakultät für Informatik, Institut für Wissens- und Sprachverarbeitung, 2004.

[58] Stefan Kramer. *Relational Learning vs. Propositionalization: Investigations in Inductive Logic Programming and Propositional Machine Learning*. PhD thesis, Technisch-Naturwissenschaftliche Fakultät, Technische Universität Wien, Austria, 1999.

[59] Stefan Kramer and Eibe Frank. Bottom-up Propositionalization. In James Cussens and Alan M. Frisch, editors, *Proceedings of the Work-in-progress track of the Tenth International Conference on Inductive Logic Programming (ILP), CEUR Vol. 35*, 2000.

[60] Stefan Kramer, Nada Lavrač, and Peter A. Flach. Propositionalization Approaches to Relational Data Mining. In Nada Lavrač and Sašo Džeroski, editors, *Relational Data Mining*, pages 262–291. Springer-Verlag, 2001.

[61] Stefan Kramer, Bernhard Pfahringer, and Christopher Helma. Stochastic Propositionalization of Non-Determinate Background Knowledge. In David Page, editor, *Proceedings of the Eighth International Conference on Inductive Logic Programming (ILP)*, LNAI 1446, pages 80–94. Springer-Verlag, 1998.

[62] Stefan Kramer and Luc De Raedt. Feature Construction with Version Spaces for Biochemical Applications. In Carla E. Brodley and Andrea Pohoreckyi Danyluk, editors, *Proceedings of the Eighteenth International Conference on Machine Learning (ICML)*, pages 258–265. Morgan Kaufmann, 2001.

[63] Mark-A. Krogel. A Data Mining Case Study. In Peter van der Putten and Maarten van Someren, editors, *CoIL Challenge 2000: The Insurance Company Case*. Sentient Machine Research, Amsterdam. Also a Leiden Institute of Advanced Computer Science Technical Report 2000-09, 2000.

[64] Mark-A. Krogel, Marcus Denecke, Marco Landwehr, and Tobias Scheffer. Combining Data and Text Mining Techniques for Yeast Gene Regulation Prediction: A Case Study. *SIGKDD Explorations*, 4(2):104–105, 2002.

[65] Mark-A. Krogel, Joachim Feist, Eva Lohmeier, Oliver Priebus, and Jörg Wunderlich. SAS Mining Challenge 2002 Report. In *Proceedings of the BTW Workshop of the GI-Arbeitskreis Knowledge Discovery*, pages 45–53, 2003.

[66] Mark-A. Krogel, Florian Kähne, and Christian Maron. Report for Data Mining Cup 2002. In *Reports for Data Mining Cup 2002*, pages 15–20. prudsys AG, 2003.

[67] Mark-A. Krogel, Simon Rawles, Filip Železný, Peter A. Flach, Nada Lavrač, and Stefan Wrobel. Comparative Evaluation of Approaches to Propositionalization. In Tamás Horváth and Akihiro Yamamoto, editors, *Proceedings of the Thirteenth International Conference on Inductive Logic Programming (ILP)*, LNAI 2835, pages 197–214. Springer-Verlag, 2003.

[68] Mark-A. Krogel and Tobias Scheffer. Effectiveness of Information Extraction, Multi-Relational, and Multi-View Learning for Predicting Gene Deletion Experiments. In Mohammed J. Zaki, Jason T. L. Wang, and Hannu T. T. Toivonen, editors, *Proceedings of the Third ACM SIGKDD Workshop on Data Mining in Bioinformatics (BIOKDD)*, pages 10–16, 2003.

[69] Mark-A. Krogel and Tobias Scheffer. Effectiveness of Information Extraction, Multi-Relational, and Semi-Supervised Learning for Mining Microarray Data. In Xindong Wu and Alex Tuzhilin, editors, *Proceedings of the Third IEEE International Conference on Data Mining (ICDM)*, pages 569–572. IEEE Press, 2003.

[70] Mark-A. Krogel and Tobias Scheffer. Multi-Relational Learning, Text Mining, and Semi-Supervised Learning for Functional Genomics. *Machine Learning*, 57(1-2):61–81, 2004.

[71] Mark-A. Krogel and Stefan Wrobel. Transformation-Based Learning Using Multirelational Aggregation. In Céline Rouveirol and Michèle Sebag, editors, *Proceedings of the Eleventh International Conference on Inductive Logic Programming (ILP)*, LNAI 2157, pages 142–155. Springer-Verlag, 2001.

[72] Mark-A. Krogel and Stefan Wrobel. Feature Selection for Propositionalization. In Steffen Lange, Ken Satoh, and Carl H. Smith, editors, *Proceedings of the Fifth International Conference on Discovery Science (DS)*, LNCS 2534, pages 430–434. Springer-Verlag, 2002.

[73] Mark-A. Krogel and Stefan Wrobel. Propositionalization and Redundancy Treatment. In Alexander Maedche, Kai-Uwe Sattler, and Gerd Stumme, editors, *Proceedings of the Second International Workshop on Databases, Documents, and Information Fusion (DBFusion), CEUR Vol. 124*, 2002.

[74] Mark-A. Krogel and Stefan Wrobel. Facets of Aggregation Approaches to Propositionalization. In Tamás Horváth and Akihiro Yamamoto, editors, *Proceedings of the Work-in-progress track of the Thirteenth International Conference on Inductive Logic Programming (ILP)*, pages 30–39, 2003.

[75] Nada Lavrač. *Principles of knowledge acquisition in expert systems*. PhD thesis, University of Maribor, Faculty of Technical Sciences, Ljubljana, Slovenia, 1990.

[76] Nada Lavrač and Sašo Džeroski. *Inductive Logic Programming: Techniques and Applications*. Ellis Horwood, 1994.

[77] Nada Lavrač and Peter A. Flach. An extended transformation approach to Inductive Logic Programming. *ACM Transactions on Computational Logic*, 2(4):458–494, 2001.

[78] Nada Lavrač, Filip Železný, and Peter A. Flach. RSD: Relational Subgroup Discovery through First-Order Feature Construction. In Stan Matwin and Claude Sammut, editors, *Proceedings of the Twelfth International Conference on Inductive Logic Programming (ILP)*, LNAI 2538, pages 149–165. Springer-Verlag, 2002.

[79] Huan Liu and Hiroshi Motoda. *Feature Selection for Knowledge Discovery and Data Mining*. Kluwer Academic Publishers, 1998.

[80] Christopher D. Manning and Hinrich Schütze. *Foundations of Statistical Natural Language Processing*. MIT Press, 1999.

[81] Ryszard S. Michalski. Pattern Recognition as Rule-guided Inference. *IEEE Transactions on Pattern Analysis and Machine Intelligence*, 2(4):349–361, 1980.

[82] Ryszard S. Michalski. *Machine Learning*. Morgan Kaufmann, 1983.

[83] Donald Michie, Stephen Muggleton, David Page, and Ashwin Srinivasan. To the international computing community: A new East-West challenge. Technical report, Oxford University Computing Laboratory, Oxford, UK, 1994.

[84] Tom M. Mitchell. *Machine Learning*. McGraw-Hill, 1997.

[85] Katharina Morik and Peter Brockhausen. A Multistrategy Approach to Relational Knowledge Discovery in Databases. *Machine Learning*, 27(3):287–312, 1997.

[86] Katharina Morik and Hanna Köpke. Analysing Customer Churn in Insurance Data – A Case Study. In Jean-Francois Boulicaut, Floriana Esposito, Fosca Giannotti, and Dino Pedreschi, editors, *Proceedings of the Eighth European Conference on Principles and Practice of Knowledge Discovery in Databases (PKDD)*, LNCS 3202, pages 325–336. Springer-Verlag, 2004.

[87] Katharina Morik and Martin Scholz. The MiningMart Approach. In Sigrid E. Schubert, Bernd Reusch, and Norbert Jesse, editors, *Proceedings of the Twenty-third Jahrestagung der Gesellschaft für Informatik e. V. (GI)*, LNI 19, pages 811–818. GI, 2002.

[88] Stephen H. Muggleton. Inverse entailment and Progol. *New Generation Computing, Special issue on Inductive Logic Programming*, 13(3-4):245–286, 1995.

[89] Stephen H. Muggleton and Cao Feng. Efficient Induction of Logic Programs. In Setsuo Arikawa, S. Goto, Setsuo Ohsuga, and Takashi Yokomori, editors, *Proceedings of the First International Workshop on Algorithmic Learning Theory (ALT)*, pages 368–381. Springer-Verlag/Ohmsha Publishers, 1990.

[90] Stephen H. Muggleton and John Firth. Relational Rule Induction with CPROGOL4.4: A Tutorial Introduction. In Nada Lavrač and Sašo Džeroski, editors, *Relational Data Mining*. Springer-Verlag, 2001.

[91] Stephen H. Muggleton and Luc De Raedt. Inductive Logic Programming: Theory and Methods. *Journal of Logic Programming*, 19/20:629–679, 1994.

[92] Claire Nédellec, Céline Rouveirol, Hilde Adé, Francesco Bergadano, and Birgit Tausend. Declarative Bias in ILP. In Luc De Raedt, editor, *Advances in Inductive Logic Programming*. IOS Press, 1996.

[93] Shan-Hwei Nienhuys-Cheng and Ronald de Wolf. *Foundations of Inductive Logic Programming*. Springer-Verlag, 1997.

[94] Nils J. Nilsson. *Artificial Intelligence: A New Synthesis*. Morgan Kaufmann, 1998.

[95] Claudia Perlich. A General Overview to Predictive Modeling in Multi-Relational Domains (Dissertation Overview). http://pages.stern.nyu.edu/~cperlich/home/Paper/DisOverview.pdf, 2004.

178   BIBLIOGRAPHY

[96] Claudia Perlich and Foster Provost. Aggregation-Based Feature Invention and Relational Concept Classes. In Lise Getoor, Ted E. Senator, Pedro Domingos, and Christos Faloutsos, editors, *Proceedings of the Ninth ACM SIGKDD International Conference on Knowledge Discovery and Data Mining (KDD)*, pages 167–176. ACM Press, 2003.

[97] Claudia Perlich and Foster Provost. Aggregation-Based Feature Invention for Relational Learning. Technical report, Stern School of Business, New York, NY, 2003.

[98] Bernhard Pfahringer and Geoffrey Holmes. Propositionalization through Stochastic Discrimination. In Tamás Horváth and Akihiro Yamamoto, editors, *Proceedings of the Work-in-progress track of the Thirteenth International Conference on Inductive Logic Programming (ILP)*, pages 60–68, 2003.

[99] Gordon D. Plotkin. *Automatic Methods for Inductive Inference*. PhD thesis, University of Edinburgh, Scotland, 1971.

[100] Martin F. Porter. An algorithm for suffix stripping. *Program*, 14(3):130–137, 1980.

[101] Dorian Pyle. *Data Preparation for Data Mining*. Morgan Kaufmann, 1999.

[102] J. Ross Quinlan. Induction of Decision Trees. *Machine Learning*, 1(1):81–106, 1986.

[103] J. Ross Quinlan. Learning Logical Definitions from Relations. *Machine Learning*, 5:239–266, 1990.

[104] J. Ross Quinlan. *C4.5: Programs for Machine Learning*. Morgan Kaufmann, 1993.

[105] J. Ross Quinlan and R. Mike Cameron-Jones. FOIL: A Midterm Report. In Pavel Brazdil, editor, *Proceedings of the Sixth European Conference on Machine Learning (ECML)*, LNCS 667, pages 3–20. Springer-Verlag, 1993.

[106] J. Ross Quinlan and R. Mike Cameron-Jones. Induction of Logic Programs: FOIL and Related Systems. *New Generation Computing*, 13(3&4):287–312, 1995.

[107] Luc De Raedt. Attribute-Value Learning Versus Inductive Logic Programming: The Missing Links (Extended Abstract). In David Page, editor, *Proceedings of the Eighth International Workshop on Inductive Logic Programming (ILP)*, LNAI 1446, pages 1–8. Springer-Verlag, 1998.

[108] Luc De Raedt, Hendrik Blockeel, Luc Dehaspe, and Wim Van Laer. Three Companions for Data Mining in First Order Logic. In Nada Lavrač and Sašo Džeroski, editors, *Relational Data Mining*, pages 105–139. Springer-Verlag, 2001.

[109] Peter Reutemann. Development of a Propositionalization Toolbox. Master's thesis, Albert-Ludwigs-Universität Freiburg, Fakultät für Angewandte Wissenschaften, Institut für Informatik, and The University of Waikato, Department of Computer Science, Hamilton, New Zealand, 2004.

[110] Jorma Rissanen. Modeling by shortest data description. *Automatica*, 14:465–471, 1978.

[111] David E. Rumelhart and James L. McClelland. *Parallel Distributed Processing: Exploration in the Microstructure of Cognition*. MIT Press, 1986.

[112] Gunter Saake and Kai-Uwe Sattler. *Datenbanken & Java*. dpunkt.verlag, 2000.

[113] Gunter Saake and Kai-Uwe Sattler. *Algorithmen & Datenstrukturen – Eine Einführung mit Java*. dpunkt.verlag, 2002.

[114] SAS. *Combining and Modifying SAS Datasets: Examples*. SAS Institute Inc., 1995.

[115] SAS. *Enterprise Miner Reference Help, Release 4.1*. SAS Institute Inc., 2002.

[116] Kai-Uwe Sattler and Oliver Dunemann. SQL Database Primitives for Decision Tree Classifiers. In *Proceedings of the 2001 International Conference on Information and Knowledge Management (CIKM)*, pages 379–386. ACM, 2001.

[117] Eicke Schallehn, Kai-Uwe Sattler, and Gunter Saake. Advanced Grouping and Aggregation for Data Integration. In *Proceedings of the 2001 International Conference on Information and Knowledge Management (CIKM)*, pages 547–549. ACM, 2001.

[118] John C. Shafer, Rakesh Agrawal, and Manish Mehta. SPRINT: A Scalable Parallel Classifier for Data Mining. In T. M. Vijayaraman, Alejandro P. Buchmann, C. Mohan, and Nandlal L. Sarda, editors, *Proceedings of the Twenty-second International Conference on Very Large Data Bases (VLDB)*, pages 544–555. Morgan Kaufmann, 1996.

[119] Xuequn Shang, Kai-Uwe Sattler, and Ingolf Geist. Efficient Frequent Pattern Mining in Relational Databases. In Andreas Abecker, Steffen Bickel,

Ulf Brefeld, Isabel Drost, Nicola Henze, Olaf Herden, Mirjam Minor, Tobias Scheffer, Ljiliana Stojanovic, and Stefan Weibelzahl, editors, *Proceedings Lernen – Wissensentdeckung – Adaptivität (LWA)*, pages 84–91, 2004.

[120] Ehud Y. Shapiro. *Algorithmic Program Debugging*. MIT Press, 1983.

[121] Ashwin Srinivasan and Ross D. King. Feature Construction with Inductive Logic Programming: A Study of Quantitative Predictions of Biological Activity by Structural Attributes. *Data Mining and Knowledge Discovery*, 3(1):37–57, 1999.

[122] Ashwin Srinivasan, Ross D. King, and Douglas W. Bristol. An assessment of submissions made to the Predictive Toxicology Evaluation Challenge. In *Proceedings of the Sixteenth International Joint Conference on Artificial Intelligence (IJCAI)*, pages 270–275, 1999.

[123] Ashwin Srinivasan, Stephen H. Muggleton, Michael J. E. Sternberg, and Ross D. King. Theories for mutagenicity: a study in first-order and feature-based induction. *Artificial Intelligence*, 85(1-2):277–299, 1996.

[124] Susanne Streuer. Weiterentwicklung des Systems RELAGGS. Laborpraktikumsbericht, Otto-von-Guericke-Universität Magdeburg, Fakultät für Informatik, Institut für Wissens- und Sprachverarbeitung, 2003.

[125] Michael Thess and Michael Bolotnicov. *XELOPES Library Documentation Version 1.2.3*. prudsys AG, 2004.

[126] Peter D. Turney. Low Size-Complexity Inductive Logic Programming: The East-West Challenge Considered as a Problem in Cost-Sensitive Classification. In Luc De Raedt, editor, *Advances in Inductive Logic Programming*. IOS Press, 1996.

[127] Vladimir N. Vapnik. *The Nature of Statistical Learning Theory*. Springer-Verlag, 1995.

[128] Celine Vens, Anneleen Van Assche, Hendrik Blockeel, and Sašo Džeroski. First-Order Random Forests with Complex Aggregates. In Rui Camacho, Ross. D. King, and Ashwin Srinivasan, editors, *Proceedings of the Fourteenth International Conference on Inductive Logic Programming (ILP)*, LNAI 3194, pages 323–340. Springer-Verlag, 2004.

[129] Filip Železný. A Bottom-Up Strategy for Tractable Feature Construction. In Rui Camacho, Ross. D. King, and Ashwin Srinivasan, editors, *Proceedings of the Work-in-progress track of the Fourteenth International Conference on Inductive Logic Programming (ILP)*, pages 62–68, 2004.

[130] Filip Železný. Efficiency-Conscious Propositionalization for Relational Learning. *Kybernetika*, 40(3):275–292, 2004.

[131] Haixun Wang and Carlo Zaniolo. Using SQL to Build New Aggregates and Extenders for Object-Relational Systems. In Amr El Abbadi, Michael L. Brodie, Sharma Chakravarthy, Umeshwar Dayal, Nabil Kamel, Gunter Schlageter, and Kyu-Young Whang, editors, *Proceedings of the Twenty-sixth International Conference on Very Large Data Bases (VLDB)*, pages 166–175. Morgan Kaufmann, 2000.

[132] Ian H. Witten and Eibe Frank. *Data Mining – Practical Machine Learning Tools and Techniques with Java Implementations*. Morgan Kaufmann, 2000.

[133] Stefan Wrobel. An Algorithm for Multi-relational Discovery of Subgroups. In Henryk Jan Komorowski and Jan M. Żytkow, editors, *Proceedings of the First European Symposium on Principles of Data Mining and Knowledge Discovery (PKDD)*, LNAI 1263, pages 78–87. Springer-Verlag, 1997.

[134] Stefan Wrobel. Data Mining und Wissensentdeckung in Datenbanken. *Künstliche Intelligenz*, 12(1):6–10, 1998.

[135] Stefan Wrobel. Inductive Logic Progamming for Knowledge Discovery in Databases. In Nada Lavrač and Sašo Džeroski, editors, *Relational Data Mining*. Springer-Verlag, 2001.

[136] Stefan Wrobel, Katharina Morik, and Thorsten Joachims. Maschinelles Lernen und Data Mining. In Günter Görz, Claus-Rainer Rollinger, and Josef Schneeberger, editors, *Handbuch der Künstlichen Intelligenz*. Oldenbourg, 3rd edition, 2000.

[137] Xiaoxin Yin, Jiawei Han, and Jiong Yang. Efficient Multi-relational Classification by Tuple ID Propagation. In Sašo Džeroski, Luc De Raedt, and Stefan Wrobel, editors, *Proceedings of the KDD-2003 Workshop on Multi-Relational Data Mining*, 2003.

[138] Jan M. Żytkow and S. Gupta. Guide to Medical Data on Collagen Disease and Thrombosis. In Petr Berka, editor, *PKDD2001 Discovery Challenge on Thrombosis Data*, 2001.

Index